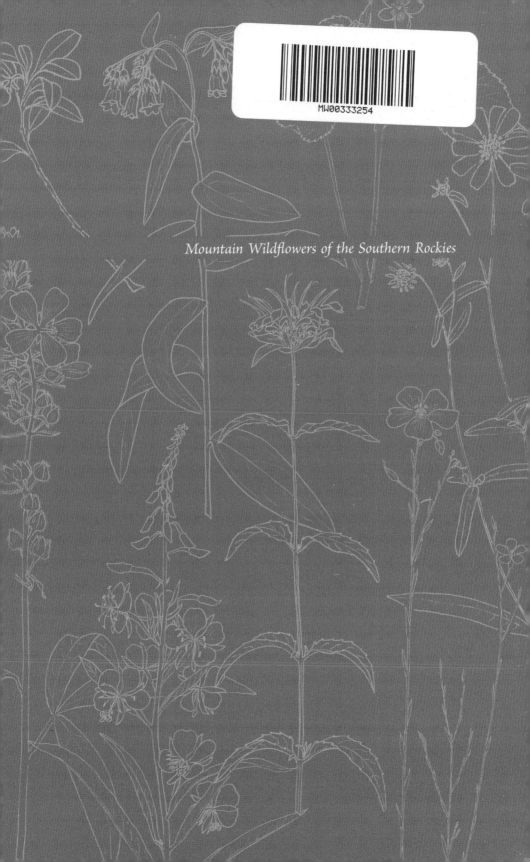

Mountain Wildflowers of the Southern Rockies

Mountain Wildflowers
of the Southern Rockies

Revealing Their Natural History

ꝼ Carolyn Dodson

William W. Dunmire ꝼ

UNIVERSITY OF NEW MEXICO PRESS ꝼ ALBUQUERQUE

LIBRARY OF CONGRESS CATALOGING-IN-PUBLICATION DATA
Dodson, Carolyn.
Mountain wildflowers of the southern Rockies : revealing their natural history /
Carolyn Dodson, William W. Dunmire.
p. cm.
Includes bibliographical references and index.
ISBN 978-0-8263-4244-7 (PBK. : ALK. PAPER)
1. Wild flowers—Rocky Mountains—Identification.
2. Mountain plants—Rocky Mountains—Identification.
I. Dunmire, William W. II. Title.
QK139.D63 2007
582.030978—dc22
2007013766

All drawings by Walter K. Graf
All photography by Carolyn Dodson and William W. Dunmire
A detailed list of photographic credits is on page 163
Book and cover design and typesetting by Kathleen Sparkes
This book was typeset using Minion Open Type Pro 10.5/13, 24p6
Display type is Brioso Open Type Pro

To Walter K. Graf

~ Some of our earliest childhood memories are following our father through the woods on a quest for nature. He was looking for wildflowers; we were fidgeting and bored, wanting to get to the next creek to turn over rocks to look for anything but "weeds." His quest, of course, was the one that prevailed and was the real reason for our visit into the wilderness. A few hours later, after being unwrapped from damp paper towels, the prized specimens of the day were placed in a small vase and then carefully and meticulously drawn. The life-size drawings took shape using the sharpest eye for detail, capturing in a most scientific manner even the smallest of fine hairs on the plants. Using an eraser was strictly *verboten*! This time spent in the evenings drawing at the kitchen table required that we three kids had to entertain ourselves very quietly, and usually we ended up deeply immersed in our own drawings.

Our father's ritual of hunting for flowers and plants not yet depicted in his ever increasing collection of numbered drawings continued for more than thirty years. After retiring from the army he moved to New Mexico, where the majority of the drawings were done, often in campsites scattered throughout the state. From orchids to cacti, from grasses to trees, the flowering plants were captured in fine line drawings. It was at this time that he started taking photographs of wildflowers, amassing a collection of over 4,000 slides. However, the drawings were always preeminent and drawn from life, never copied from the photos. His goal was to eventually end up with 1,000 drawings. Dad made it to 938 before his untimely death from ALS in 1991. Looking back on those drawings now that Raymond is a professional artist, we are amazed at the consistency over the years in the drawings' quality, detail, and general feel of their depiction. Placing a drawing from 1958 next to one from 1988 side by side, one cannot tell that there was a thirty-year span of time between them. His aim was to draw what he saw before him, and that never changed.

Of course just drawing or photographing the plants was not an end in itself. Dad joined the Native Plant Society and Wildflower Club, where he shared his passion with other like-minded enthusiasts, and he took botany courses at the University of New Mexico to learn more about identification. Dad's involvement in and support of environmental groups and concerns and his affiliations with the many local wildflower groups are a continuing source of pride and commitment for us three kids. We feel that he would have been very happy to have seen his drawings included in a publication such as this. As are we. ᴊ~

Raymond Graf
Norman Graf
Josephine Graf

Contents

Acknowledgments

Carolyn thanks systematists Timothy Lowrey and Jane Mygatt of the University of New Mexico (UNM) Herbarium, pollination biologist Philip Torchio, and author Robert DeWitt Ivey for sharing their expertise. She is grateful for the companionship of her enthusiastic hiking comrades. This book is written with love for her sons, Allan and David; and Becky, Deanna, Ross, and Risa.

Bill appreciates his long association with the UNM Herbarium and its ever-supportive staff. He feels fortunate to have been invited to coauthor this book after nearly all of the research had been completed by Carolyn.

The Southern Rocky Mountain Region

Introduction

⌐ℓ Whether you are driving over one of countless passes that crisscross the Southern Rocky Mountains or hiking along a park or forest trail, you can't help but delight in the swatches of color that seem to punctuate every mountain landscape. Indeed, in this part of the world, wildflowers native to the mountains tend to put on a more spectacular show than those of the more arid basins and plains below. From the time the snowpack melts in spring until a new white blanket again covers the ground a few plants are sure to be in flower on most every mountain acre that isn't lake, talus, or solid rock.

This book, meant for casual visitors as well as natural history buffs, will be your guide to identifying some of the most common and conspicuous wildflowers in these mountains. But *Mountain Wildflowers of the Southern Rockies* is much more than a field guide, for it presents a host of other useful and fascinating facts about selected plants, including their role in human history, relationships of flowers to birds and insects, origins of common and scientific plant names, family characteristics, strategies for survival, and plant evolution. Through the portrayals in this book we will lead you one step beyond wildflower enjoyment—to the point where you become a wildflower or even botany aficionado.

THE SOUTHERN ROCKIES

Made up of at least 100 separate ranges and stretching from Alberta and British Columbia south to central New Mexico, a distance of some 3,000 miles, the Rocky Mountains form the backbone of the upland system that dominates western North America. Here we focus on one subdivision of that geographical province—the Southern Rockies, which includes the Laramie and Medicine Bow mountains of southern Wyoming, the principal ranges in Colorado, and the Sangre de Cristo Mountains in New Mexico. Although technically not part of the

Southern Rockies, the Jemez and Sandia mountains of New Mexico are included in our coverage. Elevations range from 5,000 to more than 14,000 feet above sea level, with fifty-four peaks in Colorado exceeding that height.

Vegetation Zones • This range of more than 9,000 feet in elevation coupled with differences in slope and exposure results in great environmental diversity. Mountain plant communities vary according to latitude, exposure, and, most importantly, elevation. For each 1,000-foot rise in elevation, average temperature drops more than 3° Fahrenheit, and annual precipitation from rain and snow increases about four inches—a combination that results in more available moisture for plants during the growing season. Furthermore, average precipitation increases by about two and one-half inches every hundred miles traveled from south to north in the Southern Rockies. Available moisture, along with temperature and soil type, is key to what grows where in any particular place.

As you ascend a mountain you pass through a succession of vegetation zones that are defined by the dominant plants—in our case one or more conifers—that characterize the pattern of vegetation in a given area (see diagram). At the lowest elevations where it is warmer and dryer, piñon pines and juniper trees in an open woodland make up the coniferous overstory of the *piñon-juniper zone*. The understory of this pygmy forest tends to be grassy. East of the Continental Divide these woodlands occur only south of Colorado Springs.

Ascending in elevation, the cooler and wetter climate results in almost pure stands of ponderosa pine in the *ponderosa pine zone*. The understory becomes more shrubby. This zone extends down to the lower foothills in the northern part of our area.

Although stands of Douglas-fir trees typify the next higher life zone—the *Douglas-fir zone*—white fir (in the south), limber pine, aspen, and lodgepole pine (in the northern sector) are also major forest components. Shrubs make up much of the understory. Mixed conifer or montane are other terms applied to this zone.

Higher still, the *spruce-fir zone* is dominated by tall, dense stands of Engelmann spruce and subalpine or corkbark fir up to tree line. A heavy accumulation of forest ground litter restricts undergrowth. It is often called the subalpine zone.

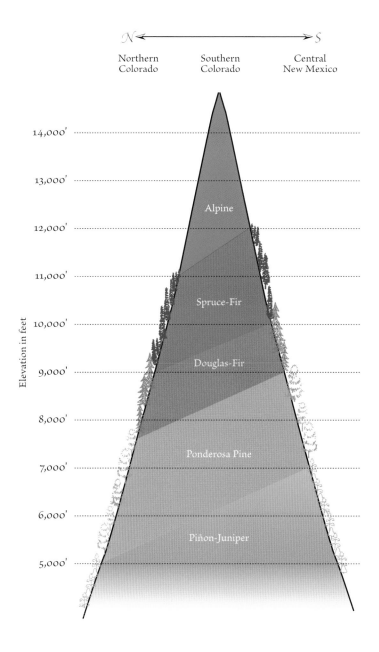

Typical elevations of vegetation zones in the Southern Rocky Mountains. The average elevation for each zone increases from north to south.

At tree line—the upper limit of the spruce-fir zone—trees are dwarf and sparse. Above are the cold, windswept, treeless slopes and mountaintops of the *alpine zone*, where vegetation is scattered and made up of low-growing plants adapted to harsh growing conditions.

The wildflower descriptions in this book include a reference to those zones where the plant is found. Although a few wildflowers can grow from the foothills to the lower summits of the Southern Rockies, the majority are restricted to one or two vegetation zones.

The Wildflowers • Well over a thousand species of wildflowers are native to the Southern Rocky Mountains. Our intent is to provide the reader a sampling of this vast flora. The seventy-five species featured herein were selected because they are both common and characteristic of the Southern Rockies, their flowers are particularly striking, they are representative of the thirty-seven plant families covered here, and they have interesting stories to tell.

USING THIS BOOK

The plants are grouped by family arranged in natural order, beginning with the most primitive families and progressing to the families that exhibit the most advanced characteristics. Each species is accompanied by a color photo taken in a natural setting by the authors, and most of the profiles include a drawing by wildflower artist Walter Graf. When you come across a plant that resembles one of the photos, check the description to see if you've got a match. If the description doesn't quite fit but, with the illustration coupled with the indicated vegetation zone, seems close, chances are that your plant is related to the described species.

Common as well as scientific names along with the plant family are given for each wildflower. Common names vary widely over geographic regions, but each plant carries only a single scientific name that is recognized the world over.

Now it's time to head for the mountains!

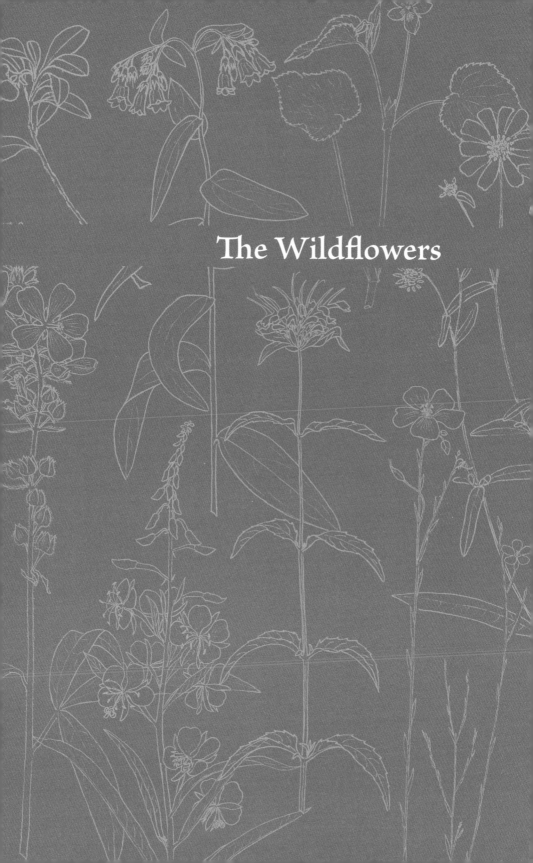

The Wildflowers

Monkshood

Buttercup Family

Aconitum columbianum Nutt.

Ranunculaceae

Amethyst flowers form a loose spike on the upper part of tall, erect stems. A cowl-shaped sepal resembling a medieval monk's hood encloses four smaller sepals as well as the petals of each inch-long flower. Lobed, jaggedly toothed leaves are five inches across on the lower part of the stem but decrease in size toward the top. Before flowering the plant is similar to larkspur in leaf shape and growth habit. Monkshood blooms all summer long in moist forest openings of the Douglas-fir and spruce-fir zones.

POISONOUS AND MEDICINAL PROPERTIES

This plant surely evokes the Middle Ages—both by the shape of its flower and in a more sinister way. Aconitine, a powerful and quick-acting poison extracted from monkshood, was put to good use in ancient and medieval times. The sixteenth-century Flemish herbalist Rembert Dodoens believed, "Aconit is of two sorts . . . the one aconit that baneth or killeth panthers, the other aconit that killeth woolfs." Wolfsbane is, in fact, an alternative common name today. The potent alkaloid that slows heart rate and lowers blood pressure was used in small doses for treating heart conditions well into the nineteenth century and is still an important medication today. Toxin from the most poisonous monkshood species may be fatal when absorbed through the skin, and florists can suffer poisoning merely by handling them. All parts of the plant are poisonous, including the below-ground tuber. An 1872 botanical textbook warns, "The root has been mistaken for horse radish with fatal results." Fortunately, ours is not one of the extremely toxic species.

Bumblebee Pollinators

Because they are deep inside the hood top, the nectaries are inaccessible to most insects. But long-tongued bumblebees are able to reach them. The bumblebee climbs up into the flower, walks over the stamens toward the nectaries concealed in the roof, and unfolds its tongue (which may be an inch long) to gather nectar and carry it in its stomach to the nest, where the nectar is disgorged. Exiting the flower, it picks up pollen from the anthers.

Vestiges of a Larger Range

Curiously, small populations of monkshood also occur in Iowa, Wisconsin, Ohio, and New York, evidence that its range extended over most of the present-day United States during the last Ice Age. When the climate warmed, monkshood disappeared from unfavorable sites, leaving distributional gaps.

An Eccentric Botanist

Thomas Nuttall, the eminent nineteenth-century naturalist, collected the first specimen of this species while accompanying John Jacob Astor's trappers to the mouth of the Columbia River. Although esteemed for his scientific contributions, he had his quirks. On one occasion when his party members were preparing to defend themselves from raiding Indians, the barrel of Nuttall's gun was found to be useless. It was packed with dirt, for he had been using it to dig up plants! Richard Dana immortalized him as "Old Curious" in *Two Years before the Mast*, describing him as "sort of an oldish man with white hair . . . who spent all of his time in the bush and along the beach picking up flowers and shells and such truck." Nevertheless, this one-time professor of botany at Harvard was an acute collector of plants and birds that were new to science.

Pasque Flower
Anemone patens L.

Buttercup Family
Ranunculaceae

Early in the spring when nearby snow may still be melting, clumps of pasque flowers protected by lacy green bracts emerge. The half dozen or so oval, petal-like sepals are lavender with silky hairs on the underside and white and shiny above. True petals are absent. In early morning the flower nods downward on its bent stem, and the sepals close together like a diminutive tulip. Under the midday sun the sepals spread out into three-inch white bowls with a center of golden stamens encircling the green pistil. After blooming, several finely dissected hairy grayish leaves develop at the base of the stem. Pasque flower may be found growing in open woods and meadows from the ponderosa pine up to the spruce-fir vegetation zone.

NAMING THE PASQUE FLOWER

Showy patches of pasque flower bloom on open rocky slopes around Easter; indeed, the name *pasque* derives from the French word for "Easter." Delicate plumes that carry the seeds off with the wind remain on the plant until midsummer, giving the appearance of smoke rising in the breeze. Prairie smoke is a name for the plant at this stage. From its resemblance to a favorite early-blooming garden flower, another popular name is prairie crocus. *Patens* means "spreading." Occurring throughout the prairie grassland as well as in the mountains, pasque flower is the floral emblem of Manitoba and the state flower of South Dakota.

A Strategy for Flower Warming

The long silky hairs on the leaves, stem, and sepals insulate the plant from the cold. Many plants protect themselves with insulating hairs, but pasque flowers also have developed a more ingenious device for keeping warm. When fully open, the white sepals form a parabola that focuses the sun's rays on the flower center, raising the temperature of this part of the plant several degrees above the surrounding air and so accelerating the development of ovules and pollen. Furthermore, this parabolic reflector attracts insects that must warm their muscles in order to fly in the cold. Seeking warmth from one flower to the next, the insects spread pollen.

A Rock Garden Favorite

Cultivated as an Easter specialty, pasque flower is a popular addition to well-drained rock gardens. This elegant flower is all the more spectacular for its habit of blooming at a time when most other plants are still dormant.

Colorado Blue Columbine

Aquilegia coerulea James

Buttercup Family

Ranunculaceae

Look for large, showy blue and white flowers on leafy two-foot stems in high-elevation rocky sites. The star formed by the five blue sepals encloses five spreading white petals that extend backward into long narrow nectar spurs. A golden center of stamens surrounds the pistil. Flowers tip upward; their spurs point to the ground. Leaves are divided into three round scallop-edged leaflets. Colorado blue columbine occurs in the Douglas-fir vegetation zone but is more common from the spruce-fir zone to above tree line.

Its status as Colorado state flower is well deserved. As one of the most attractive native flowers, Colorado blue columbine has been suggested as an appropriate emblem for the United States. Gardeners imported the plant into the British Isles in 1864 with immediate success, and it has graced English gardens ever since.

Naming This Plant

The origin of the name is lost in history, but etymologists are undeterred, and opinions on the matter abound. *Columbine* probably derives from the word for "dove" because the flower resembles five doves drinking at a fountain. Considering that the genus was initially named in Europe where floral spurs on columbines are shorter and curved, *Aquilegia* may come from the Latin for "eagle," recognizing the similarity of the spurs to talons. Hispanics capture the flower shape with the name *copa y platita* or "cup and saucer."

A Colorado Blue Relative

At lower elevations the smaller red columbine (*Aquilegia elegantula*) is festooned with crimson blooms. Unlike the Colorado blue, its flowers are pendent with the stamens hanging down. The knobbed points of the spurs may remind you of a medieval jester's cap. The red color attracts hummingbirds who, with their needlelike bills, can reach the nectar at the top of the spurs. Long-tongued bees can also collect nectar, but occasionally you see holes made in the spurs by frustrated short-tongued bees who cannot reach the nectar from inside the flower. They extract nectar through these holes, bypassing both stamens and stigma, thus failing to accomplish pollination.

Discovery of Colorado Blue Columbine

Edwin James, a twenty-three-year-old naturalist on the U.S. Army's Stephen H. Long Expedition, which sought to find the headwaters of major rivers in Colorado in 1820, collected the first scientific specimen. We can imagine his delight upon first encountering *Aquilegia coerulea* in a scrub oak thicket near Palmer Lake at the foot of the Rocky Mountain Front Range. When he published the official species description, James named it *coerulea*, for its sky blue color. Although many authors now use the more correct Latin form, *caerulea*, James's original *coerulea* is the name accepted by the Board of International Botanical Nomenclature. The official rule states that the name given with the original description of a species cannot be changed, even if it is an incorrect word form or a typographical error.

Not Always Blue

Despite James naming this columbine for its sky color, not all *Aquilegia coerulea* flowers are blue. The darkest blue flowers occur in the Southern Rockies, but in the Great Basin and on the Colorado Plateau flowers are pale blue or white. Interestingly, spur length varies with bloom color. Spurs on the darkest flowers are under an inch long, but they are up to three times longer on white blossoms. Field botanists observe that plants with dark blue, short-spurred flowers grow in regions where bumblebees are the principal pollinators; in contrast, pale, long-spurred plants thrive in places where hawk moths are the primary insect visitors. With their long tongues hawk moths extract nectar from the equally long spurs.

Marsh Marigold
Caltha leptosepala DC.

Buttercup Family
Ranunculaceae

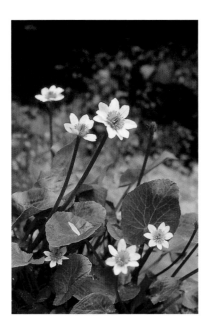

Dazzling white carpets of marsh marigold appear at the melting edge of snowbanks. Each plant bears a single bowl-shaped flower on a four-inch-tall leafless stem. Although the half dozen or more sepals resemble petals, true petals are lacking. The waxy sepals, white above and bluish underneath, surround numerous yellow stamens. Flowers emerge from basal rosettes of shiny, heart-shaped leaves that are edged with tiny scallops. Marsh marigold is common in marshy high mountain meadows of the spruce-fir and alpine vegetation zones.

NAMING THE MARSH MARIGOLD
Marigold, a contraction of "Mary's gold," honors the Virgin Mary. Marsh marigold was the name originally conferred on a yellow-flowered relative in Europe; then when the North American white species was discovered, it automatically took on this inappropriate label. *Caltha* is from the Greek for "vase-shaped basket" or "goblet"—referring to the shape of the flower. *Leptosepala* means "with narrow sepals."

PETALS, SEPALS, AND TEPALS
Flowers such as marsh marigold that bear only one set of outer floral segments pose this question: Are they sepals or petals?

By convention botanists call them sepals; or the term *tepal* is used to indicate organs not identifiable either as petal or as sepal.

As a rule, when both sepals and petals are present on a flower, they serve different functions. Green leaflike sepals enclose and protect the developing flowers, while large and showy petals draw in potential pollinators.

Adapting to Long, Snowy Winters

Mountaintops are harsh environments for plants, not least because persistent winds create deep snowdrifts interspersed with exposed, rocky soil. Beneath winter snow cover marsh marigolds are protected from dehydration and physical damage from wind and windblown particles; however, once they emerge, the plants must cope with a belated, shortened period in which to grow and reproduce. To make the most of the abbreviated summer, preformed flower buds from the previous growing season allow the plants to bloom soon after snowmelt.

The Wildflowers ❧ 9

Barbey Larkspur
Delphinium barbeyi (Huth) Huth

Buttercup Family
Ranunculaceae

Intense blue flowers are clustered atop a tall, hairy stalk. Just as the lark has a spur on the rear of each foot, larkspurs are embellished with a prominent spur on the back of each flower, formed by the largest sepal that extends back into a long nectar sac and encloses the other sepals and petals. Stalked leaves are five inches broad and divided into deeply incised lobes. Up to twenty leafy stems can emerge from a single root. In late summer masses of Barbey larkspur create azure seas in high mountain meadows of the spruce-fir and alpine zones.

Naming Delphinium

Several larkspur species occur in the Southern Rockies, all immediately recognizable by that distinctive floral shape. Plants may be a few inches to six feet tall, with flowers ranging from blue, to purple, to white. *Delphinium* is commonly thought to derive from the Greek word for "dolphin," presumably for its resemblance in bud to the aquatic mammal. Then, too, Delphinios was a common epithet of Apollo, the God of medicine, and larkspurs were used by physicians in ancient Greece. The name of this delphinium honors nineteenth-century Swiss botanist William Barbey.

Thwarting the Nectar Thieves

Floral nectar must be protected from ants and other small insects that crawl into flowers and suck up the nutritious liquid. Because their tiny bodies rarely touch either stamens or stigmas, the flower receives no fertilization service in payment for lost nectar. Larkspur sepals and

petals, however, fit together to form an impenetrable entrance—impenetrable except to brawny insects such as bumblebees with the strength to push away the barriers to reach the nectar. An insect large enough to enter the flower is large enough to contact the stamens and carry away pollen.

A Cattle Killer

The livestock industry calls larkspur the greatest killer of cattle on the western mountain rangeland. Poisoning from Barbey larkspur is so serious that in the 1930s the federal government created an extensive grubbing project to eradicate the plants from cattle ranges in western national forests. That approach wasn't entirely practical, because Barbey larkspur often grows on rough, inaccessible mountainous terrain. Aversive conditioning, where cows are fed small amounts of larkspur combined with a dose of a nauseating substance, has shown signs of promise. The cattle then associate larkspur with nausea and avoid it in the field. The lengths to which cattlemen go to avoid larkspur poisoning indicate the severity of the problem. Conversely, early settlers took advantage of the poisonous constituents and used larkspur seeds as bait poison for exterminating lice.

Unlovely Buttercup
Ranunculus inamoenus Greene

Buttercup Family
Ranunculaceae

Five glossy yellow petals surround numerous stamens on half-inch-wide, bowl-shaped flowers. The narrow petals alternate with green sepals that are tinged with purple on the underside. Lower leaves are round with rounded lobes; the upper leaves are long and narrow. Rarely more than a foot tall, this rather inconspicuous plant blooms throughout the season on moist forest floors and along stream banks, mainly in the Douglas-fir and spruce-fir vegetation zones.

Several species of buttercups occur in the Southern Rockies. Heart-leaf buttercup (*Ranunculus cardiophyllus*) has fan-shaped leaves with scalloped edges. Aquatic buttercup (*R. aquatilis*) floats on ponds and small streams and is one of the few nonpoisonous buttercups. Its flowers are white, and its leaves are divided into threadlike segments as is typical of many aquatic plants. Snow buttercup (*R. adoneus*), with exceptionally showy yellow flowers, is limited to alpine habitats.

BUTTERCUP FAMILY

Buttercup, marsh marigold, delphinium, clematis, and monkshood flowers seem to have little in common, but they do exhibit a suite of characters typical of primitive flowering plants. All have numerous stamens, free (not joined) petals, and an ovary situated above the base of the petals and sepals. This ovary is considered "superior," not in a qualitative sense but in reference to its location above, or superior to, the other flower parts. Although some family members are medicinally useful, many are poisonous to humans.

A FROGGY FAMILY

The word *Ranunculus* comes from the Latin for "little frog." Like those amphibians, buttercups are found in shady damp places. Oddly, *inamoenus* means "unpleasing." Granted, this buttercup is less showy than other species, but unpleasing seems a stretch. Crowfoot, referring to the leaf shape of some species, is another common name for buttercups.

DO YOU LIKE BUTTER?

Children love to answer this question by holding a buttercup flower under their chin and looking for a yellow reflection. The shiny petals have a waxy patina that reflects sunlight, making flowers stand out against a background of green vegetation and thus more visible to insects. Bees leave pollen on the glossy petals. Dew and rain slide off the slick surface, carrying the pollen to the stigmas below, fertilizing them. The base of each shining petal projects into a pocket enclosing a nectar-producing gland.

Grape-holly
Berberis repens Lind.

Barberry Family
Berberidaceae

This diminutive ground-hugging evergreen shrub produces bright yellow flowers in spring that develop into dark blue berries by the end of summer. Blossom clusters consist of dozens of cuplike quarter-inch flowers, each with nine petal-like organs in three whorls. Grape-holly is best recognized by its compound leaves that are composed of three to nine paired leathery leaflets having prickly hollylike margins. Its preferred habitat is dry coniferous forests where it grows in the shade—from the piñon-juniper to the Douglas-fir vegetation zone.

A close relative, Fendler's barberry (*B. fendleri*), is a four- to five-foot-tall shrub with spiny stems and simple leaves growing in the spruce-fir zone in the southern part of our mountains.

Grape-holly Names

Repens refers to the plant's creeping habit from underground stems. A plethora of common names apply to this plant. Besides grape-holly, it's known as Oregon grape, holly-grape, mountain holly, creeping mahonia, and creeping barberry.

Barberry Family

A small family of plants native to the Northern Hemisphere and South America, Berberidaceae flowers have six small yellow petals and six sepals, both of which are similar in appearance. Barberries in the Southern Rockies are evergreen and shrubby, and most have spiny leaves. The berries may be purple, blue, or red. All have bright

yellow inner wood, an obvious identification character if you peel a twig. Barberries are popular garden cultivars in the West and are frequently grown as hedges.

HUMAN USES

Settlers of the West collected grape-holly berries, which were sometimes mixed with apples, for boiling down into jelly. For Native Americans, the principal use was medicinal. The dark yellow roots and inner stem bark contain berberine, a strong alkaloid that can relieve upset stomachs and other internal pains. Boiled roots produce a yellow dye that traditional Native American craftspeople still employ for dyeing fibers from wild plants that are woven into baskets. Traditional Navajo rug weavers boil the leaves and stems for a greenish yellow hue that is applied to their wool yarn.

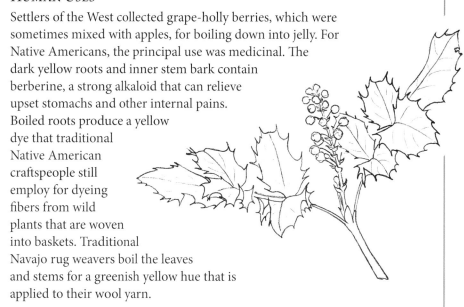

Case's Fitweed
Corydalis caseana Gray

Bleeding-heart Family
Fumariaceae

Large bushy plants display showy clusters of pink flowers at the ends of the branches. The inch-long flowers are unique, with the two outer petals flaring out at the top, one with a spur at the base. Within the outer petals are two smaller ones joined at the tips. Fernlike bluish green foliage covers the stout, succulent four-foot-tall stems. Inch-long seedpods expel their seeds explosively. Blooming in summer, this lush plant is seen along rivulets in the Douglas-fir and spruce-fir vegetation zones. Although uncommon in the Southern Rockies, where it does occur it often forms considerable patches.

Within the same upper range but extending down to lower elevations, golden smoke (*Corydalis aurea*) is a closely related species common on rocky hillsides. This leafy plant is low and sprawling, with yellow flowers having a shorter, more rounded spur than fitweed.

BLEEDING-HEART FAMILY

Dutchman's breeches, bleeding-heart, steers' heads, and squirrel-corn—these names alone suggest the varied and complex flower shapes in this largely Old World family. To access nectar, a bumblebee must crawl through the outer pair of petals and then push on the inner ones, thereby exposing the anthers and becoming dusted with pollen.

What's in a Name?

Corydalis is the Greek name for the Crested Lark, alluding to the resemblance of the crest, or keel, on the outer petal to this European bird's crested head. When it is ingested by livestock, toxins in the plant tissue give the animals fits. Eliphalet Lewis Case, an early-nineteenth-century California amateur botanist, first collected this species.

Plant Chemistry

A poison, a sedative, and an antimalarial drug have all been extracted from Case's fitweed. Ingestion of this plant has resulted in significant livestock losses over the years, for, despite its toxicity, the foliage is palatable to both cattle and sheep.

Velvet Umbrellawort
Mirabilis melanotrichia (Standl.) Spellenburg

Four-o'clock Family

Nyctaginaceae

Brilliant red-purple flowers enhanced by five long golden stamens nod in loose clusters atop three-foot-tall erect stems. Flowers are grouped by threes in leafy cups, and as fruits mature, these cups expand into papery saucers. Oval leaves are paired along the stem, and leaves of a pair are unequal in size. Look for umbrellawort in dry forest openings in the piñon-juniper, ponderosa pine, and Douglas-fir vegetation zones.

Four-o'clock Family

Contrary to appearances, the colorful blossoms of Four-o'clock Family plants have no petals, and in compensation for the loss of these showy floral parts, sepals assume the petals' role of attracting pollinators. Instead of the typical green leaflike structures that protect developing flowers, four-o'clock sepals furnish vivid enticements that lure visiting insects. An involucral cup of undersized leaves enclosing each flower cluster provides the protective role. Leaves that are opposite and unequal in size are a distinctive family trait.

Evidence of prehistoric Indian use is abundant, and many modern tribal members still use four-o'clock roots as a cure for stomach pain, eye infection, and sore muscles among other ailments. Bougainvillea and sand verbenas (but not true verbenas) are ornamentals of this family.

Family, Genus, and Species Names

Four-o'clock Family plants are night bloomers, and *Nyctaginaceae* comes from the word for "night." *Mirabilis* is Latin for "wonderful"—so named because the genus contains a number of spectacular flowering species. *Melanotrichia*, meaning "black hairs," refers to the hairy bracts at the base of the flowers.

Nocturnal Flowers

The advantage of flower closure during the day—the time most pollinating insects such as bees, wasps, and flies are active—has been answered by pollination biologists. They conclude that nocturnal moths, though less numerous than their diurnal counterparts, can be more effective pollinators. Moths carry more pollen on their larger bodies, and because they travel longer distances, pollen is distributed over a greater area.

Pygmy Lewisia
Lewisia pygmaea (Gray) B. L. Robins.

Purslane Family
Portulacaceae

At the start of a day the low tufts of two-inch-long, fleshy leaves are hardly visible among neighboring plants. By mid-afternoon, however, the ground becomes carpeted with half-inch-wide pink flowers among the leaves. Though blooms are usually pink, they can be white or magenta. From five to twelve oblong petals are lined with dark veins with five to eight stamens in the center. Blooming from May to August, pygmy lewisia occurs on gravelly soil in forest openings in the Douglas-fir and spruce-fir zones.

A showier related plant, bitterroot (*Lewisia rediviva*), with much larger rose-colored flowers, is common in the Northern Rocky Mountains and named state flower of Montana.

PURSLANE FAMILY

Fleshy leaves and an unusual feature of only two sepals on each flower characterize this family. One species, common purslane, originally from Eurasia, has become a cosmopolitan weed pest in many parts of the world but is cultivated for its nutritious leaves elsewhere. In ancient Roman times Pliny advised wearing this plant as an amulet because of its healing powers. Notchleaf purslane was an important prehistoric food plant for Native Americans. The family also includes moss-rose and other rock garden ornamentals.

MERIWETHER LEWIS (1774–1809)

Lewisia honors Meriwether Lewis, the early-nineteenth-century naturalist who, with William Clark, explored the uncharted Northwest by boat, horse, and foot. The expedition traveled up the Missouri, across the Northern Rockies on an old Indian trail, and down the Columbia River to observe "the soil and face of the country," as instructed by President Jefferson. During the outward course of this journey Lewis made a substantial botanical collection, but unfortunately it was lost on the return trip during a canoe wreck. After the loss, he amassed 150 additional specimens that are now housed at the Philadelphia Academy of Sciences.

Moss Campion
Silene acaulis (L.) Jacq.

Pink Family
Caryophyllaceae

These delicate alpine jewels can charm even the most jaded mountaineer. Low leafy mounds are covered with half-inch-wide flowers bearing rose-pink petals that are oblong and slightly notched at the tip. Crowded with tiny, grasslike leaves, moss campion truly does resemble a clump of moss. *Acaulis* (lacking a stem) indicates that the flower stalks arise directly from the crown. Moss campion is restricted to the alpine zone where it regularly graces the tundra.

Pink Family

The common family name refers not to flower color, which in most species is white, but to another definition of the word *pink*—"to cut with indented edges," as in pinking shears. Indeed, petals are often notched, or pinked, at the tip. Leaves are opposite and narrow, and the stems enlarge at the points of leaf attachment. Carnation, baby's breath, sweet William, and moss campion are ornamentals in the Pink Family.

Alpine Plants

An abbreviated growing season, frigid temperatures, stiff winds, intense solar radiation, and rocky substrate challenge plants at high elevations. Low moisture is also a problem because snow often blows away before melting, and rain can turn to inaccessible frost in icy soil. As a result, few species are able to succeed in such habitats and only those uniquely adapted survive.

Many alpine plants hug the ground below the main force of the wind, forming low compact mounds or pincushion profiles. Dense clustering of the leaves limits water loss. Alpine plant seeds germinate in crevices where the wind has deposited small accumulations of soil and where surrounding rocks radiate some warmth. Alpine species are perennial, growing slowly during short unpredictable summers. Because plant growth, flowering, and seed set take place during the short season of above-freezing temperatures, the simultaneous flowering creates a stunning multihued carpet.

In extreme years alpine plants remain virtually dormant and may even have to shed some branches for lack of resources to maintain the plant through an especially severe winter. Yet once established, they may survive for years, and some alpines may live longer than humans.

Of course conditions harsh for vegetation are harsh for pollinating insects as well. Flies are the most common visitors to mountain heights, but they, too, are adversely affected by cold and wind. Plants compete for scarce pollinators with colorful bowl-shaped flowers containing nectar that is easily accessible to any passing insect.

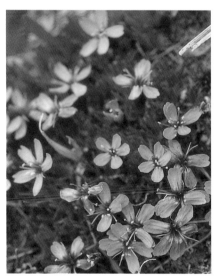

Bistort
Bistorta bistortoides (Pursh) Small

Buckwheat Family
Polygonaceae

Miniature white flowers are densely clustered in long cylindrical spikes on stems over a foot tall. Eight protruding stamens on each flower give each cluster a tufted appearance. Flowers at first appear pink, then, as the season progresses, they fade to white and eventually turn brown. Leaves up to a foot long on slender basal stalks are smooth and lance-shaped. *Bistort*, meaning "twice twisted," describes the shape of the hefty root. Swaying in the wind on their tall wiry stalks, bistort's cotton-ball-like heads can dominate the vegetation in moist high mountain meadows of the spruce-fir and alpine zones.

BUCKWHEAT FAMILY

Family members display swollen nodes along their stems, and the name *Polygonaceae* translates to "many knees." Though the flowers are small, they are deployed in dense clusters that can be delightfully showy. The display is not caused by petals, which are absent in the Buckwheat Family, but by the three to six sepals that often become enlarged after fertilization. Silver lace vine, a fast-growing ornamental often used as a screen on fences, is in this family, as is rhubarb.

Edible Buckwheats

Cultivated buckwheat, native to Eurasia, has seeds that can be ground into flour. Though not in the Grass Family and therefore not a true cereal, the seeds are processed in the same way as cereals. Rhubarb also arrived from Asia and has become naturalized in cool, wet habitats across the northern states and Canada. Boiled rhubarb stems, laced with malic acid that conveys a tart flavor, have become a true American dessert. Rhubarb leaves, however, contain oxalic acid, which makes them poisonous.

It's the starchy bistort rootstalk that has a food connection—with both American Indians and pioneers living in the West. Roasting imparts a sweet nutty flavor.

Changes to Scientific Names

Although these names are unique to each plant and are recognized everywhere in the scientific world, it's sometimes necessary to transfer a specific epithet from one genus to another. Such a change is based on evidence unavailable when the plant was named or occurs when the name was invalidly published. In either case the name of the original author (the person who supplied the specific epithet) is placed in parentheses followed by the person who determined the change. For bistort, Frederick Pursh initially placed the plant in the genus *Polygonum*, and later John Small determined it belonged in the genus *Bistorta*.

Sulphur Flower
Eriogonum umbellatum Torr.

Buckwheat Family
Polygonaceae

Slender foot-tall stalks rising from matted clumps of leaves terminate in several bright yellow (or rarely cream-colored) spheres of flowers. Each two- to four-inch cluster consists of a dozen or more tiny bell-shaped flowers having six petal-like sepals that turn rusty as they age. Spoon-shaped leaves at the woody base of the plant have blades up to two inches long and are hairy on the underside. Sulphur flower blooms from June to August in dry forest openings and rocky slopes from the ponderosa pine to the spruce-fir vegetation zone in the Colorado and Wyoming portions of the Southern Rockies.

WILD BUCKWHEATS

The genus *Eriogonum* comprises a huge and diverse group of plants, most of them growing in dry regions of the western United States. Known as wild buckwheats, they are recognized by slender branches that fork in pairs combined with clustered small white, yellow, pink, or red flowers and basal spoon-shaped, often woolly, leaves. Although the genus is readily recognizable, identification at the species level is difficult, often requiring examination of the floral structure with a hand lens. *Eriogonum* is Latin for "woolly knees," referring to the woolly stems of many species.

Food and Medicine

Wild buckwheats have long provided at least a minor source of food for Indians living in the West, as demonstrated by preserved carbonized seeds and other plant parts identified at many archaeological sites. But Native Americans seem to have placed a much greater value on the medicinal uses of these plants, at least in recent times. The ground-up roots of sulphur flower and other wild buckwheats have been associated with helping relieve stomach aches, colds, and rheumatism.

Life Medicine Plants

Sulphur flower is one of many Navajo "Life Medicine" plants that are still used in combination with other wild plants in rituals and for relieving a variety of everyday ailments. The mixture is saved for use in emergency situations or times of sickness when it often is brewed for a tea. This "medicine kit" may be used by laypeople without a ceremony, but traditional Navajos always offer a prayer before collecting a wild plant for whatever purpose. A great number of plant species may be used to concoct the various Life Medicine mixtures, although a few, including sagebrush (*Artemisia* spp.), puccoon (*Lithospermum* spp.), and several of the wild buckwheats, regularly top the list.

St. Johnswort
Hypericum scouleri Hook.

St. Johnswort Family
Clusiaceae

Bright yellow starlike flowers bloom in open, round-topped clusters. Tiny black dots line the margins of the five yellow petals. Long stamens in five bundles surround the prominent pistil, and buds are tinged with red. The showy flowers lack nectaries, but copious pollen draws in bees. Opposite, inch-long leaves are oval and spotted with black oil glands that appear translucent when held against the light. This two-foot-high bushy plant is encountered in wet meadows and along streams in the ponderosa pine and spruce-fir zones.

St. Johnswort Family

Opposite leaves dotted with oil glands and stamens grouped in bundles characterize this chiefly tropical family, which is represented in our area by a single genus. Mangosteen and mamay are highly prized tropical fruits.

Wort is the Old English word for plant. St. Johnswort was named for St. John the Baptist, whose birthday is celebrated on June 24 when the plant typically puts forth its yellow blooms.

A Noxious Weed

Klamath weed (*Hypericum perforatum*) is a larger, more robust St. Johnswort with narrower leaves, more branches on each plant, and numerous flowers in a broad, flat-topped cluster. A noxious weed introduced from Europe, it was first spotted near the Klamath River in 1900. It rapidly spread over western rangeland and became a serious problem for ranchers, crowding out native vegetation. A toxin in the plant tissue causes photosensitivity in grazing animals resulting in severe skin irritation and eventual blindness. This toxin also causes potential insect predators to avoid the plant, allowing it to spread aggressively. Today the weed is controlled by a beetle introduced from the plant's native habitat. The larvae's habit of avoiding the upper leaf surface protects them from the effects of the toxin.

Natural History of Weeds

Weeds are exquisitely designed to invade new territory. They typically produce enormous numbers of seeds with efficient dispersal mechanisms. Minuscule weed seeds travel long distances on the wind; are able to germinate in a variety of soil, moisture, and light conditions; and then rapidly mature to the flowering stage. Their unspecialized flowers can be pollinated by most insects. Though many weeds favor disturbed soil, they can invade and propagate successfully in diverse conditions. After a time, however, native plants more fully adapted to a specific habitat usually become reestablished and outcompete the invaders.

Medical Uses for St. Johnswort

A tea of St. Johnswort leaves has been used for centuries as an antidepressant in Europe, and in Germany the herb continues to be a favored therapy of psychiatrists for depression. The herb increases the serotonin activity in the brain and has few side effects.

White Checker Mallow
Sidalcea candida Gray

Mallow Family
Malvaceae

Long spikes of white or cream flowers atop three-foot-tall leafy stalks are the very image of a close relative, our garden hollyhock. The five petals have irregular margins and prominent veins. Numerous stamens join at the base to form a tube bearing bluish pink anthers that surround the style. Lower leaves are four inches across, nearly round, and have seven coarsely toothed lobes; upper leaves are smaller with linear lobes. White checker mallow is found in moist mountain meadows from the ponderosa pine to the spruce-fir vegetation zone.

NAMING WHITE CHECKER MALLOW

When Asa Gray, America's leading botanist in the mid-1800s, realized that these plants resembled both genera *Sida* and *Alcea*, he combined those names to form the new genus *Sidalcea* and called the species *candida*, which means "white." *Mallow* is from the Latin for "soft," perhaps referring to the softness of the leaves.

MALLOW FAMILY

A column of stamens in the flower center like a fountain spraying out dozens of colored droplets is a unique feature of this easily recognizable family. The mature ovary resembles a cheese wheel that splits into sections. Hairs covering the soft leaves and stems are star-shaped with branching lobes. The leaves are typically maplelike with a few large lobes. Insects are attracted by the nectar, which is secreted by hairs on the inner surface of the sepals.

Economic Plants of the Mallow Family

Seeds of the genus *Gossypium* have especially long, tough hairs. Farmers in four widely separated regions of the world, recognizing the value of the strong hairs for weaving, began cultivating cotton more than 4,000 years ago. Four wild species were domesticated—two in the New World and two in the Old—but American upland cotton, originally developed as a crop in central Mexico, proved superior and makes up most of the cotton grown for fabric today. *Gossypium* seeds yield cottonseed oil as well as a high-protein residue, cotton cake, used as cattle feed.

The fruits of wild globe mallows were widely eaten in the prehistoric Southwest, and the fruit of another family member, okra, a native of Africa, is an important vegetable in some parts of the world. Marshmallow, the candy, was made from the mucilaginous sap of marshmallow plant roots but now is manufactured from sweetened egg whites. The garden ornamentals hibiscus, hollyhock, and rose-of-Sharon are in this family.

Canada Violet

Viola canadensis L.

Violet Family

Violaceae

Patches of low plants with white flowers glittering among heart-shaped leaves can carpet a damp forest floor. Five unequal petals display purple lines and are yellow at the base; the larger lower petal extends back into a nectar sac. Tufts of hairs around the flower center provide footholds for visiting insects and prevent drops of water from rolling into the heart of the flower, thus diluting the nectar. Canada violet blooms in early summer.

With flowers ranging from violet, to blue, to yellow, to white, violets are recognized by their unique petal arrangement and heart-shaped leaves. A smaller violet common in the Southern Rockies is the mountain blue violet (*Viola adunca*). The nectar spur of these little gems is curved (*adunca* means "hooked" or "curved"). Both species thrive in the Douglas-fir and spruce-fir vegetation zones.

Violet Pollination

The fragrant violet flowers accommodate an assortment of insect pollinators. After landing, a visitor follows the dark guidelines on the petals to the nectar. Larger insects such as bumblebees clasp the flower and push their heads into the corolla tube, thrusting their tongue into the spur. This displaces the stamens, causing pollen to deposit on the bee's abdomen. Smaller insects land on the front petal and must turn upside-down to reach the nectar. They then carry the nectar away on their backs.

Closed Flowers

Should insects fail to appear when flowers are ready for pollination, the plant has a second chance for producing seeds before the end of the season by falling back on specialized flowers that never open. Within these green, inconspicuous buds that lack petals and nectar, stamens fertilize the ovules. This self-fertilization ensures that in a year of scarce pollinators, the plant will still produce seeds.

Seeds Planted by Ants

Mature violet seeds are ejected from the seed capsule with a force that may land them several feet from the mother plant. Foraging ants, attracted by the oily, nutritious appendage on each seed, carry them back to their colonies. In the anthill they devour the oily lobe, leaving the seed intact. Then, neat housekeepers that they are, the ants discard the seeds in the colony refuse pile. The process benefits both the ants, who receive nutritious oil-rich food, and the plants, whose seeds are sown in fertile soil, hidden from seed-eating mice.

    The dependence of violets on ants is demonstrated in South Africa, where native ants feed on violet seed oil. But today these ants are being displaced by invading ants with different food habits, resulting in a dramatic decrease of wild violet populations.

A Host of Human Uses

Violet flowers can be made into jelly, syrup, or candy. Furthermore, the high vitamin C content in young leaves and flower buds can furnish a nutritious addition to raw salads. *Viola odorata* is grown in the south of France for essential oils used in the manufacture of perfumes, flavorings, toiletries, and the sweet liqueur *parfait amour*. A range of bright colors and monkey-facelike petals make pansies and johnny-jump-ups favorite garden ornamentals.

Rocky Mountain Beeplant
Cleome serrulata Pursh

Caper Family
Capparaceae

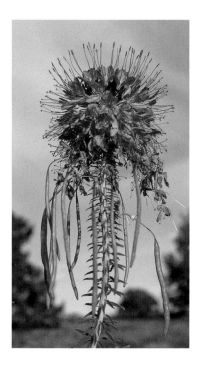

Tall bushy plants bearing round three-inch clusters of delicate lavender flowers grow along roadsides and in other disturbed places. Long green-tipped stamens that protrude from each tiny four-petaled flower give the clusters a feather-ball appearance. Slender long-stalked seedpods dangle from the flowers. With three bluish green leaflets, beeplant leaves emit an unpleasant odor when crushed. Blooming throughout the summer, Rocky Mountain beeplant is limited to the piñon-juniper and ponderosa pine vegetation zones.

Perfectly Named

Beeplants are chiefly pollinated by bees attracted by the copious nectar. In fact, beekeepers often cultivate beeplants to maintain their honeybee hives. *Capparaceae* comes from the Latin word for "billy goat," alluding to the unpleasant goatlike odor of many family members. *Serrulata* refers to the finely serrate or sawlike leaf margins.

Caper Family

Principally composed of tropical trees, the Caper Family is represented in our area by only a few herbaceous species. It resembles the mustards, a closely related family with four petals and six unequal stamens; however, Caper Family leaves are compound with three to seven leaflets, and the flowers bear four to many long stamens. Capers, enjoyed in a salad or as fish seasoning, are the pickled flower buds of a shrub native to the Mediterranean region. The ornamental spider flower, a close relative of beeplant, has a leggy, spidery look to its long stamens and stalked petals.

A Plant of Many Uses

Beeplant seed and pollen found in coprolites (desiccated human feces) at archaeological sites indicate that beeplants provided a major source of food for prehistoric Native Americans. Calling it "Indian spinach," Pueblo Indians in New Mexico still boil up the young, iron-laden plants, removing the bitter flavor and bad smell in the process.

The most distinctive use—both prehistoric and modern—of Rocky Mountain beeplant is the manufacture of black pigment for painting pottery. A concentrate of boiled leaves is dried and formed into little

cakes that are reconstituted to yield a black pigment that the designer paints upon an unfired pot. Today if you buy "traditional" ware with black designs from a Puebloan potter, you are getting a pot that has been handcrafted and patterned with beeplant paint.

Heart-leaved Bittercress
Cardamine cordifolia Gray

Mustard Family
Brassicaceae

Massive patches of miniature white flowers clustered atop two-foot leafy stems grow along mountain streams and in moist meadows. The four-petaled flowers are half an inch wide. Long-stalked heart-shaped leaves with scalloped edges are indented at the base. Inch-long seedpods are slender and slightly flattened. Heart-leaved bittercress blooms in July in the Douglas-fir and spruce-fir vegetation zones.

The name *Cardamine* is derived from the Greek word *kardamon*, referring to a Persian or Indian herb with pungent leaves. *Cordifolia* means "heart-shaped leaf."

MUSTARD FAMILY

Four petals combined with four long and two short stamens are distinctive, making this an easily recognized family. Because of the similarity of flowers among the many Mustard Family genera, species identification is frequently based on the great variation in seedpod forms. Fortunately, the pods form quickly so that a single plant often bears both flowers and fruit. Pod shapes may be cylindrical, needlelike, rounded or flattened, spherical, heart-shaped, spectacle-shaped, curved, twisted, and with or without a beak at the tip.

BITTERCRESS AND SHADE

Bittercress occurs much more frequently in the shade of willows or at the edge of a spruce forest than in the open sun. Seeking an explanation for this, Colorado botanists coupled their knowledge that plant-eating insects are more common in sunnier places with the fact that plants in these sites are water stressed compared with those in shadier areas. They determined that the water-stressed leaves of bittercress contain a lower concentration of the mustard oils that repel many insects, concluding that a major factor in the shade distribution of bittercress is protection from plant-eating insects.

Western Wallflower
Erysimum capitatum (Dougl. ex Hook.) Greene

Mustard Family
Brassicaceae

Round clusters of yellow flowers top two-foot-tall branchless stems. The four petals narrow down to a thin strap, or claw, at the base, forming a Maltese cross. Erect narrow seedpods are about three inches long. As the stem lengthens, buds are continually produced at the top, and new seedpods develop below each flower cluster. Lance-shaped toothed leaves alternate along the stem. Western wallflower is at home from the piñon-juniper to the spruce-fir zone. It blooms from spring until the end of the season.

At higher elevations western wallflowers can be orange or even maroon, with fewer blossoms per plant. *Erysimum* is from a Greek word meaning "to help or save," indicating that the ancients used the plant for medicine.

Cultivated Mustards

Oils in mustard leaves and stems defend plants against bacteria and fungi as well as leaf-eating insects and mammals. By happy accident some of the compounds that repel plant predators are tasty to humans, and thus many Mustard Family plants are grown for food, including rutabaga, watercress, radish, horseradish, cabbage, and, of course, mustard.

The ancient Greeks were the first to cultivate local forms of wild cabbage. During the Middle Ages variants were selected and grown for their expanded leaves (kale and collards), large compacted leaf heads (cabbage), small compacted heads borne in the axils of each leaf (Brussels sprouts), thickened stems with terminal dense flower buds (broccoli and cauliflower), and bulbous stems (kohlrabi). These vegetables are varieties of a single species, *Brassica oleracea*. In addition to food for humans, the family provides fodder and oilseed crops, as well as ornamentals such as alyssum and candytuft.

DAVID DOUGLAS (1799–1834)

Western wallflower was originally described by David Douglas, an early-nineteenth-century professional gardener who was sent by the Horticultural Society of London to the United States to collect plants suitable for cultivation in England. In the course of eleven years he undertook three journeys to the far West, where he collected thousands

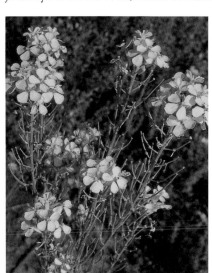

of botanical specimens. Tragically, at the age of thirty-five he succumbed to a freak accident in Hawaii on the slopes of Mauna Loa, where he fell into a pit and was gored to death by a bull. He is remembered for his discovery of Douglas-fir, along with fifteen other conifers and many flowering plants.

Bearberry

Arctostaphylos uva-ursi (L.) Spreng.

Heath Family

Ericaceae

Dry rocky forest floors are sometimes carpeted with this prostrate, mat-forming shrub. Pea-sized flowers—pink, waxy, and urn-shaped—hang from the woody branches like miniature bells. Its shreddy-barked stems are covered with oval, leathery inch-long erect evergreen leaves. The pale flowers, blooming from May to July, are less conspicuous than the bright red berries that mature in late summer. Spreading branches may extend ten feet or more. Bearberry has an extensive vertical range in the Southern Rockies, providing occasional ground cover from the ponderosa pine up to the alpine zone.

Heath Family

Woody plants with leathery evergreen leaves are typical of this family. Although many of them inhabit moist, boggy habitats with acid soil, this family also includes the beautiful red-barked madrone trees and manzanita shrubs of the West. Heather, rhododendron, azalea, and mountain laurel are among the ornamentals. Blueberries, cranberries, and huckleberries are commercially cultivated heaths.

Repetitious Names

The scientific and common names for bearberry are triply redundant. *Arctostaphylos* is from ancient Greek roots referring to "bear" and "berry"; *uva-ursi* is Latin for "grape-bear." And indeed, bears do relish the berries. Meriwether Lewis, on the Lewis and Clark Expedition, noted, "The natives eat the berries without any preparation. They are sometimes gathered and hung in the lodges in bags." Lewis also remarked, "The natives smoke its leaves mixed with tobacco." In fact, kinnikinnick, an alternative common name for this plant, is an Indian word for tobacco.

A Legendary Medicine Plant

Although the somewhat tasteless berries once supplemented the diets of numerous Indians, bearberry leaves, with their antiseptic, diuretic, and anti-inflammatory constituents, have played a much more important role in human history. Bearberry leaf teas have long been used, in both Europe and North America, for treating bladder, kidney, and urinary tract disorders, and leaf concentrates are key ingredients for many herbal medicines and food supplements.

A Unique Family Feature

You can observe a unique character of Heath Family stamens with a hand lens. Inside the corolla the swollen top of each pollen-producing anther is drawn out into two long narrow tubes. As the anthers mature, pollen is squeezed out of the tubes like toothpaste; then, when an insect enters the flower, the sticky pollen is positioned to adhere to its body.

Bog Wintergreen
Pyrola asarifolia Michx.

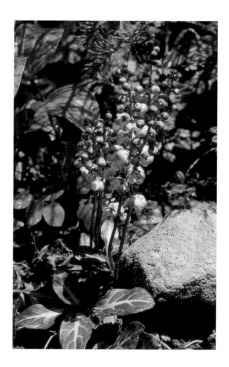

The foot-tall slender stalk of this handsome plant bears a dozen or so pale pink flowers in open whorls. Small narrow sepals enclose five waxy pink petals forming a bell-like, nodding flower. The thick curved style is longer than the petals. Round leathery basal leaves are two inches across and finely toothed. Borne on narrowly winged stalks, they are brownish beneath and dark green above. Look for this plant on shaded ground in the Douglas-fir and spruce-fir vegetation zones.

WINTERGREEN NAMES

Both elements of the botanical name refer to leaf form. *Pyrola* means "little pear," in reference to the similarity of its leaves to those of pear trees. *Asarifolia* refers to leaves like those of wild ginger. Another common name, shinleaf, possibly derives from the early use of wintergreen leaves in making plasters for shin abrasions. The original source of wintergreen oil is spicy wintergreen, a close relative that grows in eastern North America.

WINTERGREEN FAMILY

Closely related to the Heath and Indian Pipe families, the Pyrolaceae is a small family of around forty species restricted to cooler parts of the Northern Hemisphere. The several Wintergreen Family species occurring in the Southern Rockies are small inconspicuous plants of the forest with basal rosettes of dark green, leathery leaves. The flowers are waxy and sometimes exceedingly fragrant. Prince's pine or pipsissewa (*Chimaphila umbellata*) has clusters of white flowers on a six-inch stem with long, toothed leathery leaves. Sidebells (*Orthilia secunda*), under four inches tall, has white flowers arranged along one side of a curved flowering stalk; on the other hand, the flowering stalks of western wintergreen (*Pyrola chlorantha*), a plant of the same size, are erect. Woodnymph (*Moneses uniflora*) differs from the others by having only one flower on each stalk. Pleasantly fragrant, it is white and nearly an inch wide.

Pinedrops
Pterospora andromedea Nutt.

Indian Pipe Family
Monotropaceae

Bell-shaped flowers hang from the top third of a two-foot-tall unbranched, asparagus-like stem. Scattered scales below the flowers represent vestiges of leaves. Sticky hairs cover the stalks and the five long red sepals that enclose pink flowers. *Pterospora* means "winged seed," alluding to the minute wind-dispersed seeds of this genus. Pinedrops are common in dry ponderosa pine and Douglas-fir zone forests, their stiff hairy stalks persisting through the winter.

Saprophytes

Most plants manufacture food from sunlight, carbon dioxide, and water. A few, however, have evolved a different strategy to obtain nutrients. These plants are easy to spot because they are leafless and never green. Some, like pinedrops, are saprophytes, obtaining complex nutrients from decaying organic matter in the soil. Their underground stems form a compact mass enveloped by fungal strands that break down the organic matter and pass sugars, along with minerals and water, to the saprophyte host. Freed from the burden of manufacturing food, saprophytic plants only emerge above ground to flower and set seed. They can grow on the floor of dark forests where sun-dependent plants cannot, but their pollination cycle and seed dispersal are identical to those of their green relatives.

Protocarnivorous Plants

The snapping jaws of Venus flytraps and the insect-dissolving fluid deep inside pitcher plants fascinate kids and adults alike. Carnivory is a survival mechanism for plants growing in nitrogen-deficient soil whereby this essential element from their elaborately trapped prey is absorbed.

Pinedrops and other protocarnivorous species have an advantage over other plants in situations where soil nitrogen is scarce. These plants immobilize insects and other small herbivores by

trapping them in sticky stem glands and then release enzymes that digest the animal protein and incorporate the amino acids in their tissues. A trapped insect quickly stimulates enzyme secretion, capturing the nitrogen before insectivores steal the prey.

Shooting Star
Dodecatheon pulchellum (Raf.) Merr.

Primrose Family
Primulaceae

Resembling celestial shooting stars, several inch-long pink or magenta flowers dangle from a slender stem. The clustered stamens hang down in a pointed structure like a comet's head, with the petals sweeping back for the tail. White and yellow pollen sacs encircle the base of the petals. Long straplike leaves arise from the base of the foot-tall (or more) flowering stem. Shooting stars create glorious swatches of pink in moist meadows and along streamsides from the ponderosa pine to the spruce-fir vegetation zone.

A related species, *D. ellisiae*, grows only in the mountains of central New Mexico and southeastern Arizona. It's a more delicate plant with white petals and toothed leaves.

SHOOTING STAR NAMES

Dodecatheon refers to the twelve major Greek gods, but why the ancients used this name for a flower is obscure. *Pulchellum* means "small and beautiful." One common name, birdbills, relates to the pointed cone made by the stamens. Showy cyclamen, a related

Old World ornamental, has a similar flower configuration, thus an alternative common name for shooting star is American cyclamen. Okanogan Indians of eastern Washington State call it "curlew's bill."

Buzz Pollination

When you hear the buzzing of bees in a field of shooting stars, you are listening to pollination activity. The upswept petals and long showy stamens signal to bees that the flower is nectarless and that ample pollen remains within the anthers. To obtain this pollen, bumblebees wrap themselves around the anthers and vibrate their bodies to shake the pollen out onto their abdomens. About 10 percent of flowering plant species employ "buzz pollination."

Primrose Family

The Primrose Family is distinct from the unrelated Evening-primrose Family, with its unfortunately similar name. As a rule, primrose flowers have five petals that open during the day; in contrast, evening-primrose flowers are four-petaled and open around dusk.

Parry's Primrose

Primula parryi Gray

Primrose Family

Primulaceae

Purplish red flowers in a loose cluster top stout, foot-tall stems. The five richly colored petals form a slender tube that flares out into five lobes with a yellow ring surrounding the opening. Fleshy oblong leaves are basal, up to a foot long, and exude an unpleasant resinous odor. Those who venture up to the spruce-fir and alpine vegetation zones will delight in colorful patches of Parry's primrose growing along high mountain streams, usually within sight of melting snow.

Within four years of its discovery by Charles C. Parry in 1861, this attractive and easily propagated plant appeared in nursery catalogs. Today numerous species of *Primula* are desirable garden or house plants.

Fertilization in the Primrose Family

At an 1861 Linnean Society meeting Charles Darwin described a unique character of *Primula* flowers. Within the same species some flowers have anthers on long stalks and the stigma on a short one. In others the stigma is high and the anthers low, near the bottom of the floral tube. Pollen from the two flower types is carried by an insect on different parts of its body. Thus, pollen from tall anthers is deposited on tall stigmas, whereas pollen from short anthers is deposited on short stigmas. Though this feature had long been noticed, Darwin was the first to show its adaptive significance in preventing selfing, or fertilization with pollen from the same flower. He noted that outcrossing, or fertilization by pollen from a different plant, leads to more robust offspring, although the genetic basis for this fact would not be understood until the next century.

CHARLES C. PARRY (1823–1890)

The year that Darwin spoke to the Linnean Society on fertilization in the Primrose Family, Charles C. Parry came across his primrose in Colorado and, recognizing it was new to science, sent a specimen to Asa Gray at Harvard. He would have dug it up and then pressed it flat between two sheets of absorbent paper to dry for a permanent specimen. When Asa Gray received the specimen he compared it with others in the Harvard herbarium, determined the plant was a new species, and named it after its collector.

Parry studied botany under John Torrey at Columbia College Medical School. After receiving his M.D. degree, he joined a government geological survey of the Northwest as surgeon-naturalist. Then he worked several years as a botanist with the Mexican Border Survey, followed by a position with the Railroad Survey in Colorado. Once Parry discovered the Rocky Mountains, he returned every summer, contributing more than any other person of his day to the understanding of plant life in these mountains.

Rose Crown
Rhodiola rosea L.

Stonecrop Family
Crassulaceae

Showy congested round heads of miniature pink flowers top ten-inch-long leafy stems. Five sharply pointed petals are a quarter of an inch long. The stem is crowded with overlapping slender, fleshy leaves that have prominent midribs on the underside. After the first frost, leaves and stems turn a brilliant red. Rose crown grows in high boggy or rocky meadows and tundra.

A related species, king's crown (*Rodiola integrifolia*) that also inhabits rocky high-elevation terrain, has a flat maroon-colored floral cluster. Its flowers are smaller than those of rose crown, its leaves are oval rather than narrow, and the underside midrib is less visible.

LATIN AND COMMON NAMES

Rosea means "rosy-flowered," and *integrifolia* alludes to the entire (neither toothed nor divided) leaves. The two species are commonly referred to as king's crown and queen's crown, and they positively do resemble chessmen.

STONECROP FAMILY

Stonecrop is a family of succulent herbs, many of which are native to hot, dry regions of South Africa. The family is named for the rocky habitat of many species. *Crassulaceae*, from the word for thick, refers to the fleshy leaves of many of these species. When water is abundant, succulents take up the moisture and store it in their leaves, enabling them to survive during dry seasons. These plants often have waxy surfaces, which reduces water loss. The family has little economic value except as a source for ornamentals such as jade plant, hen and chicks, echeveria, and kalanchoe—all favorites in rock gardens. In some species, such as those kalanchoes known as air plants, plantlets develop along the leaf margins, drop to the ground, and root.

Leaves

Leaves provide energy for plants by transforming sunlight energy into sugars. Yet, though all leaves function in this way, they differ in form according to habitat. Large leaves on plants growing in shady places allow the absorption of more sunlight; smaller leaves of plants in hot, sunny habitats prevent overheating and excessive water loss. Waxy and hairy surfaces reduce water loss, and leaf hairs can also reflect solar radiation, limiting overheating.

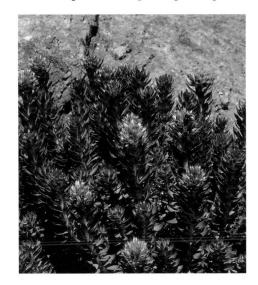

Diamondleaf Saxifrage
Saxifraga rhomboidea Greene

Saxifrage Family
Saxifragaceae

Round clusters of petite flowers atop eight-inch-tall leafless stalks rise from basal rosettes of diamond-shaped leaves. Individual cuplike flowers have five white petals, five green sepals, and ten yellow stamens. At first the dense inflorescence is a tight cluster resembling a snowball, and at that stage the plant is often called snowball saxifrage. As the stout stalk, covered with long white hairs, lengthens, the inflorescence becomes looser. The two- to three-inch leaves are thick and bear blunt teeth. At lower elevations diamondleaf saxifrage blooms in open meadows and rocky slopes in early spring; by August it will be found blooming in similar habitats of the spruce-fir and alpine zones.

Saxifrage Family

These plants are herbaceous with basal leaves and a leafless flowering stalk bearing small five-petaled flowers. They are natives of cooler regions, and some grow as far north as any plant can survive—on the north coast of Greenland. Many dainty Saxifrage Family plants, including coral bells and astilbe, adorn home rock gardens.

Saxifrage means "rock breaking." Because saxifrages grow in rocky crevices, it was assumed that the name alluded to the plants' ability to fracture rocks. But after consulting the old herbals, plant historians found that saxifrage plants were once used for treating kidney stones.

EDWARD LEE GREENE (1843–1915)

The first diamondleaf saxifrage specimens were collected in the San Francisco Mountains of Arizona in 1889 by Edward Lee Greene, one of the more controversial characters to study plants of the West. While serving as a priest in Colorado, New Mexico, and California in the latter half of the nineteenth century, he found the time to collect and describe new plants.

Eventually botany became his passion, and he left the ministry to devote himself to that field. He caused confusion in botanical literature by his habit of naming every plant variety as a different species; nevertheless, his detractors had to admit that he was one of the best field botanists of his day.

Wild Strawberry

Fragaria vesca L.

Rose Family

Rosaceae

White saucer-shaped flowers punctuate these low-lying trailing plants. Five petals surround a center of yellow stamens. Three oval leaflets are toothed along the upper half. The juicy red fruits are prized by hikers for their intense flavor, yet they are rarely seen, because wild mammals and birds usually find them first. Blooming in early summer, wild strawberries are common in meadows and on coniferous forest floors from the ponderosa pine to the spruce-fir zone.

Several species of strawberry are native to the Southern Rockies and can be distinguished in the field by differences in leaf shape and texture. Strawberries propagate by stolons (long slender red runners that creep along the soil surface) that send down roots at intervals and produce new shoots. In fact the word *strawberry* comes from the Anglo-Saxon, referring to the habit of strewing their runners over the ground. *Fragaria*, from the Latin for "fragrant," refers to the sweet floral aroma.

Our supermarket strawberry is a hybrid from two American species that were originally crossed in France in about 1750.

ROSE FAMILY

Flowers of this large economically important family of herbs, shrubs, and trees are usually showy with five free petals and numerous stamens. Most flowers are white or bright yellow, though a few have pink or red petals. The sepals, petals, and stamens attach at the base to a cuplike structure. Although Rose Family flowers share those basic similarities, the family manifests a diversity of seed dispersal mechanisms. Light, small seeds are wind dispersed; those with feathery plumes are carried farther. Members of other genera enclose their seeds in sweet, fleshy fruit, enticing wildlife and humans to eat the fruit and then discard the seeds far from the mother plant.

ROSE FAMILY CULTIVARS

Most orchard fruits grown in temperate regions, including apples, cherries, peaches, apricots, plums, pears, and quinces, are products of the Rose Family. These were domesticated from wild species in Asia or the Middle East thousands of years ago. With rose, pyracantha, bridal wreath, photinia, and other familiar ornamentals, this family is well represented in many modern temperate-region gardens.

Silverweed Cinquefoil
Argentina anserina (L.) Rydb.

Rose Family
Rosaceae

Loose clusters of saucer-shaped yellow flowers are borne on weak stems. Five petals surround numerous stamens. Compound leaves have a dozen pairs of sharply toothed, ovate leaflets covered with long silky hairs on the lower surface. Plants reproduce by red runners that can be up to six feet long. Look for them in meadows from the ponderosa pine to the spruce-fir zone.

Argentina is Latin for "silver," referring to the silky silvery leaves. Carl Linnaeus named the species *anser* from the Latin for "goose," and an alternative common name is goose grass.

CINQUEFOILS

Several cinquefoils, commonly referred to as potentillas, are native to the Southern Rockies. Because of their five yellow petals, cinquefoil flowers can be mistaken for buttercups. They differ, however, in having five leaflike bracts below the sepals along with toothed leaflets. Leaflets may be arranged in featherlike pairs along a stem or may all attach to the stem at the same place resembling fingers radiating out from a hand. The word *cinquefoil*, French for "five leaves," dates from the time when petals were thought of as leaves.

Cataloging the Plants of the World

From earliest times people recognized different kinds of plants and learned their culinary and medicinal uses as well as their dangers. Among the first written accounts are ancient Greek herbals compiled by and for physicians, classifying plants according to their medicinal properties. Subsequently Romans used these herbals, adding native plants along with their local names. In the Middle Ages, as the herbals were carried to all parts of Europe, more plants were added. Then, during the Age of Discovery, ships returned from all corners of the world, flooding European museums with exotic plants needing identification and classification.

With the influx of so many new plants, the 2,000-year-old Greek system soon proved inadequate. Dozens of new cataloging systems were proposed, but none was an improvement until finally in 1753 Carl Linnaeus published his hierarchical cataloging scheme for all known plants. He classified flowering plants into families on the basis of the number and other features of stamens and pistils. Botanists found this system far superior to all others. Although Linnaeus admitted that his hierarchical system was artificial, he was unable to devise an arrangement that represented the natural order of plants.

A century later the scientific community accepted Darwin's theory and began classifying plants according to their natural relationships. Plants are placed into families in which all members share a common ancestor. Related species within the family are grouped into genera, again with shared ancestry. The basic unit is the species—defined as a set of plants that can interbreed and produce fertile offspring.

Wild Rose
Rosa woodsii Lindl.

Rose Family
Rosaceae

Wild rose displays the shrubby growth, prickles, and sharply toothed ovate leaflets of our familiar cultivated roses. Only the flowers differ, being limited to five round, pink petals that surround numerous yellow stamens. Although the flowers produce no nectar, abundant pollen attracts insect pollinators. The fruit is a bright red or orange fleshy rose hip. Blooming from May to July, dense thickets of wild rose are found in dry, open areas from the foothills to near timberline but are more common at the lower and middle elevations.

Economic Uses

Roses are the most popular and widely cultivated flowers in the world. Wild roses have five petals and many stamens, but most cultivated roses are "double," that is, they have more than five petals. The additional petals are modified stamens, so that extremely double flowers have few or no functional stamens and thus cannot reproduce by seed. Today more than 5,000 cultivars of double roses, developed from centuries of selection and hybridization, are available in all colors but blue.

Rose hips are the richest known natural source of vitamin C, and extracts are sold in health food stores most everywhere. When World War II prevented Great Britain from importing citrus fruit, hips were gathered by schoolchildren from wild rose thickets and processed into syrup to prevent scurvy. Tasty but sour, rose hips are dried for tea or cooked into jam and jelly.

ATTAR OF ROSES

Since ancient times oil from the damask rose, native to Asia Minor, has been distilled to yield attar of roses, the fragrant essential rose oil used in cosmetics. Today this rose is extensively cultivated for its oil. We enjoy these fragrant oils for their pleasant scents, but, more important, they play a significant role in attracting pollinators.

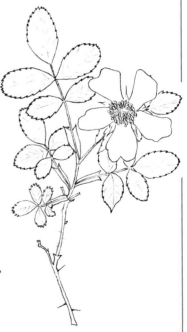

Missouri Milkvetch

Bean Family

Astragalus missouriensis Nutt.

Fabaceae

Clusters of reddish purple flowers combined with silvery foliage distinguish this low-growing plant. Sweetpealike flowers consist of five petals, with the largest one, known as the banner, ornamented with a white V-shaped spot. Four-inch-long leaves are divided into a dozen or so pairs of leaflets, with a single leaflet at the tip. Long white hairs cover the weak, prostrate eight-inch stems as well as the leaves, giving them a silvery tint. Blooming on rocky slopes in early spring, Missouri milkvetch is common in the piñon-juniper and ponderosa pine vegetation zones.

MILKVETCHES AND LOCOWEEDS

The large *Astragalus* genus includes milkvetches that provide good forage for livestock and wildlife, as well as poisonous locoweeds. All have pealike flowers and compound leaves with an odd number of leaflets. Many can be identified by the size and shape of the seedpod. Species with large dry pods are called rattle weed. The foliage of many locoweeds contains a poisonous alkaloid that affects the brain of horses and cattle, disorienting them and causing them to stagger and act "loco." Other locoweeds selectively extract toxic heavy metals such as selenium from the soil and incorporate it in their tissues, creating problems for any herbivore that chooses to nibble on them.

Soil Indicator Plants

Certain plants, termed indicator plants, thrive only on soils of specific composition. Their presence indicates a specialized local soil condition, and a map of their distribution can guide mining engineers to ore and mineral sources. Uranium prospectors, for example, exploit the ability of some *Astragalus* species to thrive in uranium-rich soil. Other species help selenium miners locate this valuable element.

Plants as Clean-Up Artists

Environmental engineers employ plants that can absorb and tolerate poisonous substances to clean up toxic waste sites. Bracken fern, for example, removes arsenic from contaminated soils and incorporates the poison into its tissues. Then the toxin-laden vegetation can be harvested and disposed of in a safe manner. Poplars, on the other hand, absorb organic pollutants such as spilled oil and then break the chemical down into less harmful compounds that are slowly released into the air. Using plants to clean up contaminated soils has become a fast-growing technology, with the advantages that it is cheaper than traditional methods and avoids using air-polluting machinery.

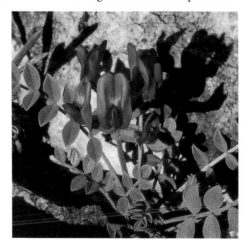

Plants able to remove heavy metals from the soil may, in the future, be put to an additional use. Chicory, when grown on gold mine waste dumps, can selectively extract enough of the precious metal to make farming for gold feasible.

Silvery Lupine

Lupinus argenteus Pursh

Bean Family

Fabaceae

Long tapering clusters of pale blue, pealike blossoms perch at the top of two-foot leafy stems. Yellow spots on newly opened flowers near the apex turn purple on the lower, older blooms. Five to nine narrow sharp-tipped leaflets covered with flat-lying silvery hairs radiate from stem tips. Fine silky hairs also cover the flat, inch-long seedpods. Silvery lupine is often abundant in dry meadows from the ponderosa pine to the spruce-fir zone.

The Lupines

As a genus lupines are easy to recognize with their whorled array of flowers combined with compound leaves with radiating leaflets—an arrangement termed palmate for its resemblance to fingers spreading from the palm of a hand. *Lupinus* derives from the Latin for "wolf," reflecting an ancient erroneous assumption that because lupine grows on poor soil, the plants are responsible for robbing soil of its nutrients. In fact it's exactly the opposite: lupine roots actually enrich soil.

The genus contains about 300 species, many of them occurring in the West, with Texas bluebonnet probably the best known. Lupine fruits and seeds contain dangerous alkaloids that affect the nervous system of sheep.

FLORAL COLOR CHANGE

The conspicuous yellow spot on freshly opened flowers attracts bumblebees to a copious supply of pollen, but after the flowers have been fertilized and the spots have turned purple, available pollen is much reduced. As bees learn this, they limit their foraging to the younger flowers.

The flowers of most plants don't change color when there is no longer a need to attract insects; they simply shed the expendable petals, freeing up maintenance energy. Lupine petals, however, continue to serve a pollination role. By remaining showy, they increase the long-distance attractiveness of the floral display to pollinators.

LEAF MOVEMENT

A notable feature of lupine leaves and those of some other plants is their movement. The leaflets of lupine are in almost constant slow motion. At night and on dark days they fold downward, enveloping the stalk like the ribs of a closed umbrella, thus reducing water loss. In sun they stand erect in a vertical position to increase incident sunlight absorption. Leaflets may rotate as much as 90 degrees during the course of a day.

Golden Pea

Thermopsis montanus Nutt.

Bean Family

Fabaceae

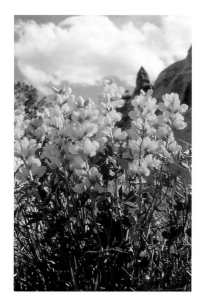

Half-inch yellow pealike flowers are clustered atop leafy one- to three-foot-tall stems. Each compound leaf consists of three oval-shaped leaflets up to three inches long. Stiffly erect three-inch seedpods are covered with dark hairs. Golden pea brightens open, dry areas such as roadsides and other disturbed places, from ponderosa pine forests up to the spruce-fir zone in spring and early summer.

Thermopsis means "lupine-like." Although similar in floral and leaf structure, golden pea is easily distinguished from lupine. Lupine flowers are pink, blue, purple, or white but never yellow in the Southern Rockies; furthermore, golden pea leaves have three leaflets, but lupine has four or more.

BEAN FAMILY

Containing about 600 genera and more than 12,000 species distributed worldwide, including trees, shrubs, vines, and herbs, the Bean Family is one of the largest. Nearly all species have compound leaves, and the seedpod is a legume—a dry capsule that can be longer than a foot or shorter than an inch, round, flat, coiled, smooth, or spiny.

BUTTERFLY FLOWERS

Papilionoid—the term for the shape of Bean Family flowers—means "butterfly-like." The largest of the five petals, the banner or standard, is showy and frequently ornamented with lines or spots; in fact, another name for golden pea is golden banner. Two smaller side petals, or wings, provide a ledge for bees to land. These three petals create the butterfly shape. Tucked between the wings, the two lower petals are joined together to form a boat-shaped structure, the keel, that encloses the reproductive structures. As a visiting bee lands on the wings, its weight releases a mechanism that allows the anthers to spring upward, resulting in pollen being sprayed onto its abdomen. Some botanists refer to this action as a tripping mechanism; thus the pollinated flower is "tripped."

ECONOMIC IMPORTANCE OF LEGUMES

Next to the grasses this widespread family is the most important source of human food and the most important provider of vegetable protein. Edible legume seeds include peanuts, lentils, peas, and beans of all types. In fact, lentils, peas, chickpeas, and vetch were among the earliest plants to be domesticated some 10,000 years ago in the Middle East. In addition, alfalfa and clover are desirable livestock fodder owing to their high protein content.

As far back as Roman times farmers recognized the restorative effects on soil through rotating Bean Family crops. Nitrogen-fixing bacteria living in nodules on legume roots convert atmospheric nitrogen into compounds essential for plant growth. Whereas most nitrogen-fixing bacteria are free-living soil organisms, this specialized association with the roots of plants in the Bean Family is the reason that farmers intercrop a field with alfalfa, clover, or soybeans. The family includes ornamentals such as wisteria, broom, and lupine. Licorice is made from the root sap of an Old World legume.

Fireweed
Epilobium angustifolium L.

Evening-primrose Family

Onagraceae

Masses of magenta fireweed flowers emblazon forest openings. Flowers in loose spikes have four petals and eight long stamens. Six-inch leaves are lance-shaped, and instead of terminating at the edges, leaf veins join together in loops. Slender three-inch pods hold numerous tiny seeds attached to long silky hairs. When the pods open, plants appear to be tipped with cotton tufts. With these feathery parachutes, the wind can carry the seeds great distances.

Fireweed thrives wherever forest clearings exist—from the ponderosa pine zone to timberline.

Angustifolium means "having narrow leaves." Young shoots are loaded with vitamins C and A, and Indians in the Northwest ate them raw or cooked like asparagus. Fireweed is the floral emblem of Canada's Yukon Territory.

EVENING-PRIMROSE FAMILY

Though fireweed is an exception, family members typically open at dusk and close by dawn, or, as John Burroughs portrays the nocturnal flower, "like a ballroom beauty it has a faded, bedraggled appearance by day." The flowers have four petals like those of the Mustard Family. There should be no confusion between these families, however, because evening-primrose petals are united into a long floral tube

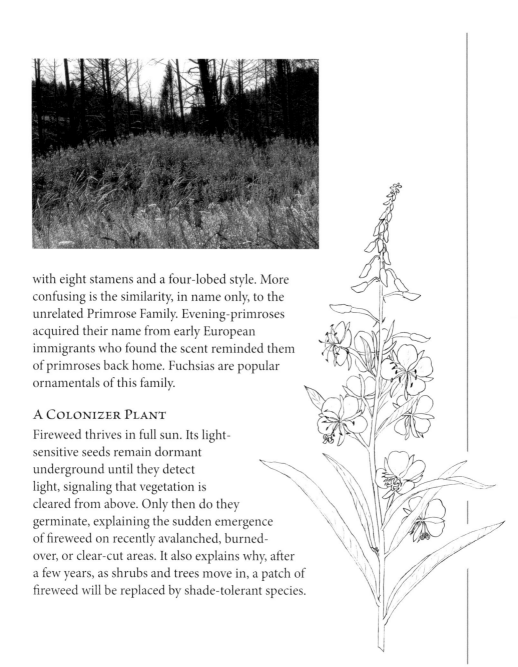

with eight stamens and a four-lobed style. More confusing is the similarity, in name only, to the unrelated Primrose Family. Evening-primroses acquired their name from early European immigrants who found the scent reminded them of primroses back home. Fuchsias are popular ornamentals of this family.

A Colonizer Plant

Fireweed thrives in full sun. Its light-sensitive seeds remain dormant underground until they detect light, signaling that vegetation is cleared from above. Only then do they germinate, explaining the sudden emergence of fireweed on recently avalanched, burned-over, or clear-cut areas. It also explains why, after a few years, as shrubs and trees move in, a patch of fireweed will be replaced by shade-tolerant species.

Hooker's Evening-primrose

Oenothera elata Kunth

Evening-primrose Family

Onagraceae

Showy flowers blooming atop three-foot-tall leafy stems are yellow upon opening and then turn orange and wither after a single day. The four petals form a long narrow tube that opens out into a bowl. Eight stamens surround a cross formed by the four long lobes of the style. Lance-shaped leaves are a foot long near the base of the stem and progressively smaller toward the top. Stems and sepals are covered with reddish hairs and give off a sweet odor at night. Hooker's evening-primrose is regularly encountered in moist meadows and roadside ditches from the ponderosa pine to the Douglas-fir zone.

Evening-primrose Medicine

Gamma linolenic acid (GLA), an essential fatty acid with therapeutic properties, is extracted from the oil of evening-primrose seeds and used to treat eczema and arthritis. Hoary evening-primrose, a North American native, is now grown commercially for pharmaceutical and dietary supplements in over a dozen countries. Botanists in the Southwest are searching for other native species high in GLA that might also be commercially propagated.

Moth Pollinators

Moths forage for nectar at dusk, after their avian predators roost. They locate night-blooming flowers in dim light by a highly refined sense of smell on their feathery antennae. Moth-attracting flowers exude a strong, sweet perfume and are usually white or pale to show up better in the twilight. Moths rely exclusively on nectar for nourishment, feeding through long hollow proboscises. Their flexible tongue is coiled when not in use; then when a moth reaches a flower, a change in blood pressure causes its proboscis to uncoil and dart forward. Moth-attracting flowers are tubular with the nectar inside—protected from the elements and accessible only to pollinators with long mouthparts.

Unlike bees or butterflies, moths take nectar while hovering in the air. The plants, relieved from having to

support the weight of an insect, can be delicate and slender. And because the only part of the moth in contact with the stamens is the thin proboscis, the pollen is presented on long sticky strings that are carried by the moth to other flowers. Thus identifying moth-pollinated flowers is easy: they are long and narrow, strongly scented, night blooming, pale, and delicate.

Blue Flax
Linum lewisii Pursh

Flax Family
Linaceae

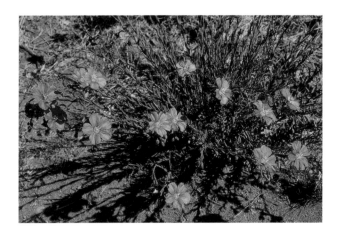

Sky blue saucer-shaped flowers wave in the breeze on slender, tall stems. Dark veins line the five delicate petals of the inch-wide flowers. The two-foot-tall unbranched stems rising from a woody base bear narrow leaves and a loose flower cluster. Stands of blue flax are splendid morning sights, but by afternoon the delicate petals have fallen, leaving only green sepals on the stems and fallen blue petals on the ground. Blue flax blooms in early summer in dry meadows from the piñon-juniper to the Douglas-fir zone.

DISCOVERY OF BLUE FLAX

When Meriwether Lewis, leader of the Lewis and Clark Expedition, first encountered blue flax he recognized that "the bark of the stem is thick and strong and appears as if it would make excellent flax." Indeed, pre-Columbian Native Americans used blue flax fiber for weaving and making fishing line. Frederick Pursh, who gave the botanical name to the plant, noted, "Flowers large, blue, a very good perennial, and it might probably become a useful plant if cultivated." Today blue flax is available in nurseries throughout the West.

AN IMPORTANT RELATIVE

Commercial flax, *Linum usitatissimum*, Latin for "most useful flax," is closely related to blue flax. One of our oldest and most important domestic plants, commercial flax has become extinct in the wild and is now found only in cultivation. Along with wheat, barley, and several legumes, flax was domesticated from wild plants by some of the world's earliest farmers between 8,000 and 10,000 years ago in the Middle East. Flax probably was originally grown as a seed crop for its edible oil rather than its fiber.

Linseed oil extracted from pressed seeds is an ingredient in the manufacture of modern paints, varnishes, linoleum, and printing ink, while the residual oil cake makes valuable cattle food. The strong, durable stem fibers are now used to manufacture linens and fine writing paper. The classical Latin name for this plant, *Linum*, gave us our words *linen* and *line*.

Medicinal Uses

Flax seeds contain prussic acid, a substance with medicinal properties. Indians incorporated blue flax seeds in their medicine kit, and European flax has long been known to have curative powers. In the eighth century no less an authority than Charlemagne decreed that flax seeds should be consumed in order to maintain good health.

Linnaeus's Clock Garden

A field of blue flax is an azure sea in the morning, but not one flower is to be seen by mid-afternoon. The flowers of

many plants open and close daily at precise times. So regular are some that Carl Linnaeus designed a clock garden employing thirteen Swedish plants. Starting at 3 AM bindweed opens, and at 10 PM the morning glory closes. By noting which flowers were open and which were closed, a surprisingly good approximation of the time of day or night could be made.

Richardson's Geranium
Geranium richardsonii Fisch. & Trautv.

Geranium Family
Geraniaceae

White flowers with lavender veins are sparsely scattered on sprawling stems. Five round petals surround the ten stamens and prominent style of each inch-wide, saucer-shaped blossom. Sepals are hidden beneath the broad petals. The large leaves are cut into deep lobes, and aromatic glandular hairs cover the entire plant. Sizable patches of Richardson's geranium are common in moist locations in the ponderosa pine up to the spruce-fir zone.

John Richardson, an early-nineteenth-century surgeon and naturalist, collected plant specimens on Canadian survey expeditions. Inhabiting dry woods, usually at lower elevations, the related mountain geranium (*Geranium caespitosum*) is easily distinguished with its reddish purple narrow petals alternating with pointed green sepals.

Geranium Family

Heron's bill, crane's bill, stork's bill—these common names for geranium flowers refer to the long pointed beaks of shorebirds. *Geranium*, too, derives from the Latin word for "crane." Upon seeing the stiff, needlelike pistil that elongates after petals have fallen, you will understand why these plants are named for a slender bird bill. Thanks to this feature, the Geranium Family is easily recognizable.

This bill-like structure provides the mechanism for dispersing and planting seeds. The long pistil splits lengthwise into five strips, each attached to a seed. When dry, the strips explosively curl up with such force as to catapult the seed with its appendage far from the plant.

There the style coils and uncoils with daily humidity changes, drilling the seed into the earth.

The family has limited economic value aside from the ever-popular houseplant, which, in addition to providing colorful blooms, yields geranium oil used in perfumes. People of various Indian tribes formerly took advantage of the astringent properties in tannin-rich wild geranium roots to control minor bleeding and to heal sores. Once listed in the U.S. Pharmacopoeia, geranium roots have since been replaced by modern drugs.

NECTAR GUIDES

The prominent veins on geranium petals (and on many other flowers as well) serve an important function in pollination. Once a bee lands on a flower, it must get its bearings to find pollen or nectar. These lines guide the bee to the nectar. Researchers have timed the length of a bee visit on a geranium where the floral lines have been obliterated with paint compared with a visit on an unpainted flower. They discovered that it takes the bee longer to find nectar on altered flowers without lines. Thus these lines, called floral guides or nectar guides, increase pollination efficiency. Often the guidelines are ultraviolet, therefore invisible to humans but glaringly obvious to bees.

TWO KINDS OF FLOWERS

Two forms of Richardson's geranium, discernable by the difference in flower size, typically occur within the same patch. The larger flowers are hermaphroditic, having both stamens and pistils and producing pollen and seeds. The smaller are female, having pistils but no stamens and producing only seeds. Female plants produce more seeds per flower than hermaphroditic ones, possibly because smaller flowers require less resource allocation than their larger counterparts.

Water Hemlock
Cicuta maculata L.

Carrot Family
Apiaceae

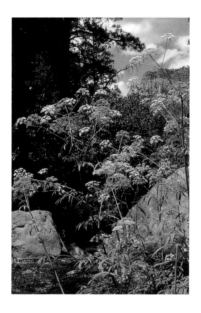

Diminutive white flowers are borne in five-inch-wide clusters on this tall stout plant. Leaves along the branching, ridged stems are divided into lance-shaped, toothed leaflets. Side veins on the leaflets run from the center to notches between the teeth, rather than to the tips of the teeth as in most plants. Water hemlock blooms through the summer in marshes and along streams at lower elevations from the piñon-juniper to the Douglas-fir vegetation zone.

Poisonous Plants

Though attractive, water hemlock is one of the most poisonous of our native species. The poison, cicutoxin, is concentrated in the tuberous roots, where minute chambers release a highly toxic liquid if the stem is broken. Anything this liquid touches can poison livestock. In spring, when cattle are first turned out to pasture, they may pull up and eat the base of the plant, resulting in violent convulsions and often death. Water hemlock should not be handled by humans, for whom as little as one-quarter of a teaspoon of the root is lethal.

Indians living in the mountainous West have long recognized that water hemlock roots are deadly. Some tribes administered carefully measured quantities of root for an emetic or used it for other medicinal purposes; others applied it to arrowheads.

Poison Hemlock

Poison hemlock (*Conium maculatum*), a closely related and even more dangerous plant, was introduced from Europe for medicinal purposes and has become naturalized throughout North America. This tall branching plant also has round clusters of small white flowers, but leaves are fernlike, and the stem shows purple spots. Universally recognized as the world's most deadly plant, it is known to scholars as the plant used by the Athenians to poison Socrates.

Queen Anne's Lace

Queen Anne's lace, an attractive garden plant native to the eastern states, is also in this family; however, its root is not only safe but edible—thus the plant is popularly known as wild carrot. Newcomers to the West, assuming they have Queen Anne's lace in hand, have sampled water hemlock's toxic root, which also has a carrot flavor. Too often the results have been fatal.

Cow Parsnip

Carrot Family

Heracleum maximum Bartr.

Apiaceae

With mammoth proportions, this giant, coarse species is the most sizable Carrot Family plant in North America. The stout, up to eight-foot-tall stem can exceed two inches thick at its base. Enormous leaves, up to a foot across, are divided into three heart-shaped, toothed leaflets. Leaves are hairy underneath, and each leaf stalk clasps the stem with an oversized sheath. Numerous white flowers are grouped in large flat-topped dense clusters. Each tiny petal is deeply cleft, and petals at the edge of the cluster are longer than those toward the center. The entire plant has a pungent odor and is palatable not only to cows but to all livestock as well as native herbivores. Patches of cow parsnip can dominate riparian vegetation from the piñon-juniper to the spruce-fir zone.

HUMAN USES

Cow parsnip was a particularly useful wild plant for North American Indians. More than fifty tribes are recorded as eating the sweet aromatic leaves and flower stalks—either raw or cooked. Yet an even greater number of Native Americans used it for medicine, ascribing different benefits for various plant parts depending on the region. Calling it *Yerba del Oso* (bear plant), Spanish settlers, too, concocted medicines from the roots to treat a variety of ailments.

Chemical Warfare

The Carrot Family provides a plethora of drugs, spices, and tasty foods. Interestingly, chemicals responsible for human medicinal benefits and culinary delights serve no purpose for plant growth or reproduction. They were considered mere by-products of plant biochemistry until less than a century ago, when the mystery of their existence was solved. Immobile plants, unable to escape from herbivores, resort to chemical warfare by producing secondary compounds in their tissues that repel, sicken, or kill their enemy—or, in some cases, mimic an insect hormone that interferes with growth. Insects, of course, fight back. They may develop enzymes to disassemble the toxic compounds. Some insects sequester poison in special cells, effectively neutralizing the toxin by isolation, and, in turn, use these poisons against their own enemies.

As insects develop protective measures to resist plant poisons, plants evolve new toxins. Ecologists term this escalating warfare "the Red Queen Syndrome." As the Red Queen in Lewis Carroll's *Through the Looking Glass* remarked, "You have to run as fast as you can to stay in the same place." A plant species can only survive by continuing to fabricate new compounds to deter insects. Insects, likewise, must constantly develop protection against these new compounds.

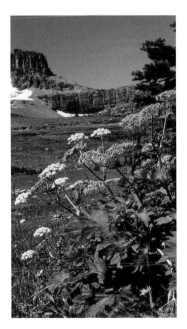

Our uses for these chemicals go beyond the medicinal and culinary. The natural insecticide pyrethrum, for example, is obtained from dried flower heads of the tansy plant.

Osha
Ligusticum porteri Coult. & Rose

Carrot Family
Apiaceae

Osha is a tall branching plant with large flat-topped compound umbels of dozens of white quarter-inch-wide flowers. Fernlike leaves up to a foot long are thrice divided into narrow, saw-toothed leaflets. The ribbed, four-foot stems are stout. These plants have a noticeable celerylike fragrance, especially after a frost. Osha is encountered in moist forests from the foothills to the spruce-fir vegetation zone.

MEDICINAL QUALITIES

Osha, the *chuchupate* of Hispanic ranchers, is a highly palatable forage plant. People of several Indian tribes identify osha with bear medicine from their observations that bears seem to seek out this plant, presumably for its medicinal properties. Before modern medicines were available, it was considered a cure-all, and even today osha is highly prized for its supposed all-purpose medicinal qualities. Ranchers have been known to tie osha sprigs to their boots to ward off rattlesnakes. It is the most widely used herbal medicine plant among Hispanics in the Southwest. Because it is so heavily gathered, osha may be disappearing from our forests.

GENERALIST POLLINATORS

Although many flowers specialize in attracting a particular kind of pollinator, flowers of the Carrot Family are generalists, attracting flies, mosquitoes, gnats, bees, butterflies, and moths. Their small open flowers present nutritious enticements on their surface, easily accessible to visitors with assorted types of mouthparts, and the tightly compacted floral heads bear the weight of large insects. At high altitudes, high latitudes, or other places where pollinators are scarce, flowers are most often generalists. Employing their generalist strategy, such flowers are more likely to attract a variety of pollinators, but with the drawback that these pollinators often fly indiscriminately from one species to another, wasting pollen that is deposited on a flower of a different species.

THOMAS CONRAD PORTER (1822–1901)

A Pennsylvania professor of botany and ordained minister, T. C. Porter traveled through Colorado and Utah in the 1870s on a government survey collecting mountain flowers. He coauthored the original *Synopsis of the Flora of Colorado*.

Mountain Parsley

Cymopterus lemmonii Gray

Carrot Family

Apiaceae

Petite yellow flowers form compact flat-topped heads up to two inches wide. Rough short hairs cover the stem just below the floral head. Smooth, finely divided leaves have a celerylike aroma. Mountain parsley is exceedingly variable, depending on habitat. Height ranges from less than a foot to three feet; leaf segments can be threadlike or lance-shaped; flower color varies from yellow to purple. These plants are often abundant in aspen groves or coniferous forest openings from the ponderosa pine to the spruce-fir vegetation zone.

CARROT FAMILY

This family is readily recognized by the compound umbel inflorescence. In an umbel arrangement, flower stalks arise from a common point at the tip of the stem much like umbrella ribs, and flowers open in sequence with the outer ones unfolding first. A compound umbel is formed of small umbels arranged in a large umbel. Leaves are usually fernlike, and swollen leaf bases wrap around the ribbed stem. Identification of the numerous species of this big family can be difficult, often depending on characteristics of the tiny seeds.

Carrot Family plants are often aromatic, thus many Old World species have been cultivated as salad herbs. Parsley, cilantro (the leaves of coriander), and dill are grown for their fragrant leaves. Those with pungent seeds include anise, caraway, coriander, dill, and fennel. Celery is the swollen, ribbed leaf stalk of yet another family member, and carrot and parsnip round out the root crops. All were domesticated before the time of Christ from wild species growing in the Mediterranean region.

JOHN GILL LEMMON (1832–1908)

Following his service in the Civil War, Michigander John Lemmon moved west, where he botanized up and down the Pacific slope. At age forty-eight he married Sara, and on their honeymoon they

climbed to the top of a mountain outside Tucson, Arizona, collecting plants along the way. Here they found the first specimen of mountain parsley. Subsequently the mountain was named Mt. Lemmon for Sara, because she was the first white woman to reach the summit. During their life together they discovered over a hundred plants new to science, leading Asa Gray to write, "Why you have *lemmonii*s as thick as locusts all round."

Monument Plant

Frasera speciosa Dougl. ex Hook.

Gentian Family

Gentianaceae

Truly a plant of monumental proportions, its stout leafy stem—sometimes as tall as a person—arises from a rosette of foot-long lance-shaped leaves that decrease in size toward the top. Two-inch-wide light green flowers form whorls in the leaf axils nearly the entire length of each stem. Narrow sepals alternate with the four broad petal lobes that surround four large stamens and a prominent pistil. Petals are spotted with purple and have a densely fringed membrane protecting two nectar glands at their base. For the first few years the plant is nothing more than a mound of velvety leaves the size and shape of deer's ears and, in fact, at this stage is commonly known by that name. Monument plant colonizes meadows and openings in the Douglas-fir and spruce-fir zones.

NAME DERIVATION

Speciosa means "showy." Older books refer to this plant as *Swertia radiata*. Three common names refer to various attributes of the plant: deer's ears, monument plant, and green gentian. The genus was named for John Fraser, an eighteenth-century English nurseryman who collected plants in North America.

LATIN NAME CHANGES

The binomial name assigned to each species is unique to that plant. But these names can change, much to the consternation of the user. New laboratory or field studies may reveal that what was considered a single species is really two or that two species thought to be distinct more validly are one. The Latin name is then changed to reflect the new interpretation. The previous name becomes a synonym, no longer valid but retained to locate the species in older botanical literature. When two botanists independently name a plant, the first name published is valid, and the second, a synonym. In this case *Swertia radiata* is a synonym of *Frasera speciosa*.

Synchronized Flowering

A monument plant's leafy stage can span several years—up to twenty or more—before the fleshy root has stored enough starch to send up a flowering stalk. After a single flowering the plant dies, leaving only a straw-colored stalk that may persist for several seasons.

In some summers nearly all plants in a colony may bloom concurrently, creating a dramatic forest of green gentians. More often only a few flowering stalks appear. The unpredictable flowering is a predator-avoidance strategy, because flower-eating insects depend on patches of flowers that are reliable every year and ignore sporadic bloomers like monument plant. But when these plants bloom in profusion, they attract a variety of insect pollinators.

A bumblebee, the principal pollinator, lands on the petals with its head pointing toward the pistil. Its tongue pushes under the hairs above the nectaries and sips from each; at the same time the anther brushes pollen onto the insect's abdomen.

Fringed Gentian
Gentianopsis thermalis (Kuntze) Iltis

Gentian Family
Gentianaceae

A solitary, vase-shaped flower tops each eight-inch stem. A delicate fringe borders the four deep blue petals, which are twisted, nearly obscuring the flower opening. Two-inch lance-shaped leaves are paired along each stem. Fringed gentians frequent mountain meadows of the Douglas-fir and spruce-fir zones, sometimes growing in such profusion as to create magnificent expanses of brilliant blue in late summer.

GENTIAN FAMILY

Plants in this family have paired, simple leaves, but, depending on the species, their flowers have either four or five united petals. Gentians' typical deep blue hues translate into some of the most stunning late summer floral displays in the Southern Rockies.

The family is named for King Gentius of Illyria, who was thought to have discovered the medicinal attributes of these plants in the second century B.C. According to legend, the king was called on to put an end to a plague. Not being a physician, yet possessing great abilities as an archer, he shot an arrow into the air and declared it would land on a cure for the disease. Apparently the punctured gentian did play a role in ending the sickness—not surprising, as medicinally useful chemicals have since been extracted from gentian leaves and roots. In fact, an Egyptian papyrus containing a medical prescription for gentian makes clear that the medicinal properties of these plants were known long before King Gentius's time.

Naming the Fringed Gentian

We owe the scientific name, *Gentianopsis thermalis*, to two botanists. Karl Kuntze collected the first specimen in present-day Yellowstone National Park during his globe-encircling botanical tour in the late 1800s. When he published his description of this new plant, he named it *Gentiana thermalis* in recognition of its thriving near many of the extraordinary thermal springs that characterize the region. Indeed, a few decades later fringed gentian was named the official flower of the park. Much later, American botanist Hugh Iltis determined that the plant was more closely allied with the genus *Gentianopsis*, but older books retain the original generic label.

Thief Protection

Twisted petals, hairs, and fringes account for the gentian's graceful flower shape. More significant, the ornamentation helps deter smaller insects. An ant or tiny beetle climbing up from below cannot get a firm grip on the fringed corolla margin to pull itself up into the flower. Preventing these nectar thieves from drinking nectar is valuable to the plant because their bodies are too small to transfer pollen.

On cloudy and rainy days the petal lobes wrap tightly around each other, forming a pointed cap that keeps out rain that might dilute the nectar and render it ineffective in attracting pollinators.

Showy Milkweed
Asclepias speciosa Torr.

Milkweed Family
Asclepiadaceae

Pink star-shaped flowers clustered in three-inch-wide spheres define this tall coarse plant growing on roadsides and other disturbed sites. Five sharply pointed corolla lobes bend backward, and the center of each flower supports an intricate petal-like crown. Spiny plump seedpods split open in late summer to liberate numerous seeds—each attached to long silky hairs. Large oval leaves are paired along the woolly white stems. A common weed of lower elevations, it blooms all summer long.

A CROWN OF NECTAR CUPS

A crown of five nectar cups perches atop each milkweed flower. In the center of this crown the pollen is packaged in pairs of waxy balls joined by straps in a saddlebag configuration. When an insect lands on the nectar cup, clawing frantically for a foothold, a leg will slip into the tiny slit between the cups and hook onto a pair of pollen balls. Then, after devouring nectar, the visitor flies off with the pollen saddlebags attached. Strategically placed hooks on the next milkweed flower snag the pollen balls and deposit them on the pistil.

This ingenious method of pollen transfer, so beneficial to the plant, is not always advantageous to the insect. Occasionally you come across the pathetic sight of an insect leg in a milkweed flower— one that had become stuck in the pollen slit and then detached as the insect flew off.

Milkweed Milk

Networks of canals embedded in milkweed leaves and stems store milky latex under pressure. Injure a leaf or stem, and white sap oozes out. Exposure to air quickly converts the latex into glue that will gum up the mouthparts of plant-feeding insects. Not surprisingly, most plant eaters give milkweeds a wide berth, simply because the sticky sap makes it impossible to consume the foliage. But caterpillars of the monarch butterfly will snip the main canal to release the latex and lower the pressure in the system, preventing the fluid from welling out when the caterpillar chews on a leaf.

Milkweed Poisons

Having solved the sticky latex problem, a caterpillar confronts cardiac glucosides in milkweed tissues. Though these barriers deter most insects, monarch caterpillars feed exclusively on milkweed without ill effect. That's because they seal off the poison in specialized cells, thus making themselves unpalatable to predators throughout their life span. The first time a bird devours a monarch caterpillar or butterfly, it suffers violent vomiting and rarely is tempted to try another one. Birds also pass up viceroy butterflies because they mimic the monarch's color pattern, although their tissues are poison free.

From Weed to Cash Crop

Traditionally considered a nuisance by farmers, milkweed has many potential uses. Indeed, in referring to the long silky hairs of the seedpod, Peter Kalm, a colonial botanist, noted in 1772 that "the poor collect it and with it fill their beds, especially their children's." During World War II our government used milkweed floss, which is more buoyant than cork, in life jackets, obtaining it by recruiting children to gather the pods from roadside plants. Today, market testing is under way for using waterproof milkweed fiber in clothing and comforters, because it is less expensive than feathers. And, finally, farmers in Utah are now investigating the feasibility of growing and harvesting milkweed latex as a substitute for petroleum.

Scarlet Gilia

Ipomopsis aggregata (Pursh) V. Grant

Phlox Family

Polemoniaceae

Showy red funnel-shaped flowers hang in elongated clusters on slender two-foot stalks. The inch-long blossoms open out into five recurved lobes that are spotted with yellow. Basal rosettes of finely divided leaves appear the first year of these biennial plants, which in the following year give rise to flowering stalks with gray-green narrowly segmented leaves. Sticky glands covering the stems and leaves emit a disagreeable skunklike odor. Scarlet gilia grows in dry openings and blooms from May to August. Expect to find it in the ponderosa pine and Douglas-fir zones.

A Multitude of Names

The various Latin names given to this gilia over the years reflect its complex taxonomic history. The first specimen was collected in 1806 in northern Idaho by the Lewis and Clark Expedition and arrived back in St. Louis as a mere "wretched scrap," according to the botanist who determined it was a species brand new to science. He gave it the binomial name *Cantua aggregata*. Further research two decades later revealed its relationship to the established genus *Gilia*, thus the name was changed to *Gilia aggregata*. More recently it was determined that the plant belongs in the genus *Ipomopsis* on the basis of morphological, chromosomal, and biochemical evidence. Other common names include ruby honeysuckle, skyrocket, and hummingbird flower.

HUMMINGBIRDS LOVE SCARLET GILIA

The flaming red tubular flowers are magnets for hummingbirds, and a mass of these plants in bloom becomes a virtual hummingbird garden. Scarlet gilia is a favorite nectar source for migrating Rufous Hummingbirds returning along the Rockies to their wintering grounds in Central America.

NATIVE AMERICAN USES

Scarlet gilias were certainly known to Indians and, later, to European settlers long before the Lewis and Clark Expedition collected that "wretched scrap" of a specimen. Assuredly, both Indians and settlers recognized most local plants, named them, and knew their uses. Hopi hunters ate the dried blossoms for good luck in hunting antelope, aware that pronghorn regularly browse upon it. Indians in the Northwest used the leaves to treat venereal diseases and for other medicinal purposes, prompting a 1940s federal government laboratory study on mice that suggested a possible antibacterial function of the dried plant material. Nothing came of it, however.

Jacob's Ladder
Polemonium foliosissimum Gray

Phlox Family
Polemoniaceae

Leafy stems exceeding a foot tall bear open clusters of blue or, less frequently, white blossoms. The funnel-shaped corolla with five round petal lobes and five yellow stamens is half an inch wide. Each narrow leaf consists of numerous lance-shaped leaflets in a ladderlike arrangement. Glandular hairs on the stems and leaves exude a skunky odor that is responsible for an alternative common name, skunkleaf. Jacob's ladder frequents moist meadows and streamsides in coniferous forests up to the Douglas-fir zone.

Related Species

Showy Jacob's ladder, *Polemonium pulcherrimum*, occurs at higher elevations. The weak stems of this plant are under a foot tall, the leaves are smaller, and the flowers are light blue. This spreading plant inhabits the spruce-fir and alpine zones, but the real mountaineer among polemoniums is sky pilot, *P. viscosum*. Dense clusters of deep violet, bell-shaped flowers bearing orange anthers adorn these low, tufted alpine tundra plants. Clumps consist of several leafy flowering stems crowded by numerous erect compound leaves. Each leaf is congested with bundles of tiny leaflets that spread out in different planes. *Viscosum* means "sticky," referring to the glands covering the foliage that emit a foul odor. Sky pilot regularly delights hikers in alpine meadows and boulder fields.

Phlox Family

Petals of the bell- or funnel-shaped flowers are joined into a narrow tube that opens out into five lobes and is enclosed at the base by an equal number of sharp-pointed united sepals. The diversity of colors and shapes in this family attracts an assortment of pollinators, with various flowers depending on bees, flies, butterflies, hummingbirds, and bats for their pollination. Gilia, phlox, and collonia are cultivated for garden ornamentals.

INSECTS ABOVE TREE LINE

Alpine tundra is a challenging environment for plants and insects alike, and sky pilot is well adapted to contend with rough mountaintop weather and thin soils. But to survive and reproduce above tree line, the plant faces another problem—that of available insect pollinators. Although its flowers are precisely accommodated to attract bumblebees, bumblebees cannot adapt to alpine conditions. Sky pilot would be unable to extend its range beyond that of its principal pollinator were it not for a floral structure modification. Below tree line sky pilot attracts bumblebees with broadly flared, sweet-smelling flowers. But in the alpine zone, where bumblebees are scarce and flies are more abundant, the flowers are smaller and narrower and emit the fetid odor that brings on the flies.

FLORAL FRAGRANCES

Jacob's ladder produces a succession of floral fragrances during the reproductive cycle. In bud and after fertilization the blossoms have that insect-repelling smell of the stems and leaves. But in full bloom a perfumy aroma attractive to insect pollinators is released. Thus, by altering the emitted odor these flowers protect themselves from plant-devouring insects during their vulnerable stages; yet when the flowers have mature pollen and receptive stigmas, they beckon pollinators with cloying sweetness.

Alpine Forget-me-not
Eritrichium nanum (Vill.) Schrad. ex Gaudin

Forget-me-not Family
Boraginaceae

Bright blue (occasionally white) flowers are clustered on two-inch-high stems arising from a tightly matted dwarf cushion. A raised yellow ring at the center of each five-petaled flower announces to an insect visitor where to insert its proboscis. The yellow ring disappears after pollination, signaling the absence of pollen. Half-inch-long lance-shaped leaves are covered with loose silvery hairs. This alpine gem is at home on exposed gravelly ridges at the highest elevations.

The Greek roots of *Eritrichium* indicate "woolly hair"; *nanum* means "dwarf."

Forget-me-not Family

An arrangement of flowers on only one side of each stalk is the clearest family trait—one not obvious for alpine forget-me-not, since stems are single flowered. Stalks of other family members are more often curled up like a scorpion's tail when flowers are in bud; then, as flowers open from bottom to top, the stalks uncoil. Five petals are united to form a bell-shaped flower, usually with a raised ring surrounding the narrow floral opening. Each flower produces four hard seeds. Course hairs cover leaves and stems in most species. These traits—the coiled inflorescence, bell-shaped corolla, coarse hairy leaves and stems, and four hard seeds within each ovary—make this family easy to recognize.

Lungwort, heliotrope, hound's tongue, and forget-me-not are ornamentals. The leaves of comfrey have a mild but distinctive oyster flavor and can be eaten fresh or cooked, though they contain alkaloids that can be toxic if consumed in quantity. Comfrey is among the oldest herbal remedies for skin problems. It contains allantoin, a chemical that promotes skin repair.

Tundra Plants

Alpine forget-me-not belongs to an association of ground-hugging, shallow-rooted plants that populate the most northerly latitudes and the highest mountains—the arctic and alpine tundra plants. Tundra, a Finnish word meaning "treeless," is too cold, has too little available soil moisture, and has too short a growing season to support trees. Alpine plants are adapted to frigid temperatures, gale-force winds,

high summer solar radiation, ultrathin soils, and a paucity of insect pollinators—principally flies. This flora originated in the high mountains of Central Asia, from where it spread around the Northern Hemisphere during warm periods of the Ice Age. Today tundra plants have become stranded on mountaintop islands or in high latitudes.

Many-flowered Puccoon
Lithospermum multiflorum Torr. ex Gray

Forget-me-not Family

Boraginaceae

Bright yellow flowers are scattered among the leafy clumps of foot-tall erect stems. Narrow funnel-shaped corollas flare out into five round lobes on the half-inch-long flowers. Flat-lying bristles cover the gray-green stems and leaves. The upper leaves—up to two inches long—are conspicuously larger than the lower ones. Flowering in early summer, this species favors forest openings from the ponderosa pine to the spruce-fir vegetation zone.

Related Species

Corollas of fringed puccoon, *L. incisum*, are distinctly ruffled along the edges. The floral tube is longer and paler, and the leaves are dark green. An early spring bloomer, it grows in dry areas at lower elevations, usually no higher than the ponderosa pine zone.

Human Uses

Pueblo Indians once treated skin irritations with puccoon extract, sometimes mixed with piñon pine resin. When it is applied to injured or stressed skin cells, the tannic acid in the plant tissue causes cells to form a protective barrier. In the West, Native Americans cooked and ate the roots.

Name Derivation

Puccoon is the Virginia Algonquian word for "dye plants," and, indeed, Native Americans have manufactured blue and violet dyes from boiled fringed puccoon roots. Gromwell, originally applied to a common European species, is an alternative common name for plants in this genus. The French call them *plantes aux perles* or pearl plants, because of their pearly white seeds. *Lithospermum* means "stone seed," alluding to the four small nutlets produced by each flower. The genus is cosmopolitan except for Australia.

John Torrey (1796–1873)

Torrey, who originally named this species, was a physician and professor of chemistry at Columbia University and also the first professional botanist in the New World. He identified numerous botanical collections gathered on government expeditions and is recognized as the first American botanist to apply Darwin's theory to plant classification. Torrey Peak near Boulder is named after him, as are many plant species. He founded the Torrey Botanical Club, which is still active today, and was a founding member of the National Academy of Sciences.

Bluebells

Mertensia lanceolata (Pursh) DC.

Forget-me-not Family

Boraginaceae

Showy clusters of colorful bell-shaped flowers cascade from the tall stalks of this leafy plant. Its pink and blue flowers are broad tubes with five flared lobes. Leaves are lance-shaped with in-rolled margins—five inches long on the lower stem, gradually becoming smaller and narrower toward the top. Bluebells occur abundantly along streams and moist open places from the ponderosa pine to the spruce-fir vegetation zone.

Several species occur in the Southern Rockies, differing by flower shape and leaf characteristics. The genus commemorates Franz Karl Mertens, a German professor of botany who traveled throughout Europe in the early nineteenth century collecting plant specimens. *Lanceolata* refers to the shape of the leaves. Bluebells are sometimes known as languid ladies, for the shape of the corolla; chiming bells is another common name.

PINK AND BLUE FLOWERS

A pleasing feature of bluebells is that both pink and blue flowers are borne on the same plant. Human aesthetics aside, the two colors serve an important function. Blue flowers, loaded with nectar, attract foraging bees. After pollination the flowers no longer need pollinators, and nectar production ceases. By this time the corolla has turned from blue to pink. Bees quickly learn the floral message: "Visit only blue flowers for nectar!"

DOCTRINE OF SIGNATURES

The leaves of some bluebell species are spotted with white, similar to the mottling on lungs—thus its alternative name, lungwort. *Wort* is an Old English word meaning "plant." The name lungwort reflects a widely held concept of the Middle Ages—the "Doctrine of Signatures"—which declares that every medicinal plant displays a clue to its use. In this case leaves resembling lungs, it was presumed, indicated the plant's efficacy in treating lung diseases.

Many of our plants retain medieval names signifying their affiliation with early medicine. For example, boneset, with its leaf pairs growing together, was once employed to facilitate the knitting of broken bones. Liverworts, whose leaves are liver-shaped, were thought to cure diseases of the liver. Eyebright, whose flowers are distinguished by clear, bright centers, was used to treat eye problems. And bloodroot, with its red sap, was prescribed for blood disorders.

Giant Hyssop
Agastache pallidiflora (Heller) Rydb.

Mint Family

Lamiaceae

Leafy four-sided stems support dense spikes of pink flowers and green bracts. Tubular flowers display an erect, notched upper lip and a spreading lower one, with teeth along the edge of the largest lobe. The four stamens are longer than the corolla. Leaves are opposite, stalked, pointed at the tip, and coarsely toothed. Stems and leaves are fragrant. Giant hyssop is found in scattered stands on rocky slopes in the Douglas-fir and spruce-fir vegetation zones.

MINT FAMILY

The combination of paired leaves, bilaterally symmetrical flowers, square stems, and aromatic foliage easily identifies this family in the field. The position of each leaf pair at right angles to the pair directly above and below results in a square stem, obvious to the touch. The petals join to form a tube or "gullet" that opens out with an upper lip protecting the reproductive organs and an enlarged lower one providing a platform where insects land and gain a foothold while feeding. Another name for this family is Labiatae, meaning "lipped," referring to that flower feature. Salvias, with their range of brightly colored blooms, and coleus, bearing ornately mottled leaves, are favorite ornamentals.

Starlings place the leaves of Mint Family plants in their nests, most likely to ward off fleas and other pests with the aroma. Ancient peoples probably used mint plants in a similar fashion to sweeten their bedding and control insect pests.

Aromatic Mints

The many aromatic oils produced by Mint Family members have provided some of our most important medicines, spices, and flavorings. Basil, marjoram, oregano, rosemary, sage, thyme, and several true mints in the genus *Mentha* were selected for early cultivation in the Old World; however, the ancients valued them more for their presumed medicinal properties than for flavoring. In the New World Indians used giant hyssop for both flavoring and tea.

Adaptations for Bee Pollination

The shape of gullet blossoms enables bees to feed quickly and efficiently. A bee will land on the broad lower lip and proceed to the back of the floral tube to lap up nectar with its proboscis. During this process pollen brought in on the insect's back rubs off on the stigma. Then, as the bee leaves to fly to another plant, the anthers sprinkle more pollen on its back. Some of this pollen is carried to other flowers, but most of it will be taken back to the hive and fed to larvae.

Beebalm

Monarda fistulosa L.

Patches of two- to three-inch purple spheres of a dozen or more blossoms grace forest clearings in summer and early fall. A straight, narrow flower tube protects anthers and stigmas, and the expanded lower petals form a landing platform for pollinators. Velvety oval leaves with finely toothed margins are paired along erect square stems up to three feet tall. The foliage exudes an oregano-like scent. Extensive stands of colorful beebalm are common in ponderosa pine and Douglas-fir zones.

A PLANT OF MANY NAMES

Beebalm is also known as horsemint, for this is a stout, coarse plant. An alternative common name, bergamot, borrowed from bergamot orange of the Mediterranean, refers to the pleasing aroma of both plants. The fragrance attracts bees and butterflies but is said to repel mosquitoes. This scent led to yet another common name, wild oregano. *Fistulosa*, meaning "resembling a pipe," describes the narrow floral tube. Older books use the botanical name *Monarda menthaefolia*—having mintlike leaves.

BEEBALM MEDICINE

Nicholas Monardes was a distinguished sixteenth-century Spanish physician in Seville, where ships arriving from the New World brought plants, unknown in Europe, that had medicinal properties. He found that many of these were effective in treating formerly incurable infirmities and compiled a treatise on them titled *Joyful News Out of the New Found World*.

Of course long before then Indians knew about the medicinal properties of beebalm. Most tribes living within the plant's range employed infusions of plant parts for colds, stomach problems, fevers, and other ailments. Herbalists still collect beebalm leaves for various medicinal uses, seasoning, and brewing teas.

NECTAR AND POLLINATORS

Like most flowers, beebalm rewards insects with nectar—sap that is tailored to meet the specific needs of preferred pollinators. Specialized plant glands remove certain substances from the sap and add others such as amino acids, enzymes, proteins, alkaloids, and vitamins.

Beebalm nectar is accessible only to pollinators with long mouthparts. Some bees fit this category, along with moths, butterflies, and hummingbirds. Landing on the lower lip of a flower, a bumblebee will suck nectar through the floral tube as its head rubs against the stigma and anthers. When a butterfly lands there, its proboscis unrolls and inserts down the tube. Moths frequent these blossoms but barely touch

the flower with their proboscises, thus they carry away only a small amount of pollen. As a hummingbird pushes its bill into a flower, the fluttering motion rubs bill and head feathers against the stigma, at the same time collecting pollen from the anthers.

Giant Red Paintbrush
Castilleja miniata Dougl. ex Hook.

Snapdragon Family
Scrophulariaceae

Flame-colored spikes atop leafy stems appear to be dipped in red paint. Hummingbirds are drawn to the radiant color, but when they close in they find the actual nectar-bearing flowers are hidden among the red bracts, and only the upper tip of the narrow green flower is visible. Leaves on the lower part of each stem are slender and green. Foot-tall clumps of giant red paintbrush regularly brighten meadows and forest openings in the Douglas-fir and spruce-fir zones.

Several species of red paintbrush as well as some yellow and pink species are native to our mountains. All have brightly colored leaf bracts enclosing inconspicuous green flowers. In bestowing the genus name, Linneaus honored Domingo Castillejo, an eighteenth-century Spanish botanist. *Miniata* most appropriately means "dipped in red ink."

A Partial Parasite

Although most plants attract pollinators with colorful flowers, Indian paintbrush (the popular name for all members of the genus *Castilleja*) accomplishes it with colorful bracts and leaves. The red leaves near the top of the plant, devoid of chlorophyll, forgo photosynthesis. And the green leaves lower on the stem are too few to capture sufficient energy from the sun. Therefore, to augment its needs Indian paintbrush must resort to taking nutrients from the roots of neighboring host plants.

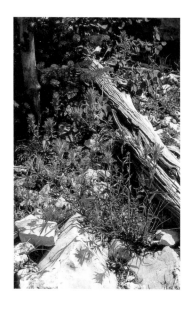

Because it is not completely dependent on hosts, botanists term it hemiparasitic or partially parasitic.

Indian paintbrush won't survive when removed from its native habitat, because digging it up separates the paintbrush from its host connection. Horticulturalists have learned to cultivate Indian paintbrush by starting it in a pot containing a grass host and then transplanting the mix to a garden, thus allowing gardeners who aren't put off by tufts of grass among their flowers to enjoy these dazzling natives.

A Complex Name Authority

The "ex" of the authors of *Castilleja miniata* indicates that the name was first proposed but not validly published by David Douglas. William Hooker later published it following botanical standards.

Yellow Monkeyflower

Mimulus guttatus DC.

Snapdragon Family

Scrophulariaceae

Luxuriant plants with bright yellow, two-lipped flowers that seem to be a cross between a pansy and a snapdragon often border mountain streams. The flower, with a large lower lip dotted with red spots, is more open than most in the Snapdragon Family. Two ridges run along the lower lip into the throat. The opposite leaves are oval and unevenly toothed, and the stems are fleshy. Yellow monkeyflowers like wet feet, thus they rarely grow far from stream, pond, or spring. Spindly stems may reach two feet in the foothills, but approaching timberline the plants are more compact and only a few inches tall.

Several species of monkeyflower, varying in color from yellow, to red, to lavender, are native to the Southern Rockies. The beautiful red *Mimulus lewisii* regularly attracts hummingbirds.

BEES ON MONKEYFLOWER

Nectar-producing glands in the flower throat are hidden from a visiting bee, but red spots on the landing platform guide the insect through the narrow entrance to the nectar. On the way it passes the stigma, where pollen is brushed from its body. After being touched, the stigma closes up, opening a passageway to the anthers. There pollen is deposited on the hairy body as the bee laps up nectar.

MONKEYFLOWER NAMES

The flower shape and red spots bring to mind a grinning face, giving rise to the names monkeyflower and *Mimulus*, Latin for "buffoon." *Guttatus* means "speckled." Indians and early settlers ate the fresh leaves uncooked; in fact, one common name is wild lettuce.

NAME AUTHORITY

The complete scientific name of every plant is followed by the name (usually abbreviated) of the person who first described the plant—in this case Augustin DeCandolle, an early-nineteenth-century botanist. The scientific community considers a proposed new name only

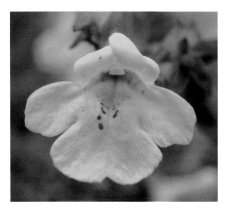

after the author has published a description of the plant and has specified where the specimen is stored. Other botanists can then examine it and determine whether the plant is, indeed, a new species.

Owl-clover

Orthocarpus luteus Nutt.

Snapdragon Family

Scrophulariaceae

Club-shaped yellow flowers protrude among leafy bracts at the top of foot-tall stems. The half-inch-long flowers are wider than they are long, with a bulge below the tip. Bracts among the flowers are hairy with linear, pointed divisions. Stem leaves are long and narrow. Owl-clover blooms abundantly in dry meadows throughout the season from the ponderosa pine to the spruce-fir zone.

Despite its name, owl-clover is not a clover; nor is it even related to clovers, which are in the Bean Family. *Orthocarpus* means "straight fruit," referring to the straight seedpod. *Luteus* means "yellow."

SNAPDRAGON FAMILY

Flowers in this large family display many sizes, shapes, and colors to match specific bee, wasp, fly, moth, or hummingbird pollinators. The five petals are joined at the base and open into two lips. The upper protects reproductive structures, and the lower may provide a landing platform. The blossoms of Snapdragon Family plants often resemble those of the Mint Family, but there should be no confusion between the two. Most mints have square stems and aromatic foliage, but snapdragon stems are round, and their foliage is odorless. Cardiac glycosides such as digitalis produced by foxglove are important heart medicines. Beardtongue, foxglove, butter-and-eggs, slipper flower, and, of course, snapdragons are favorite ornamentals.

COLOR VISION IN BEES

When bees began to acquire food from flowers early in the evolution of both groups, flowers were dull green, and bees were color-blind. Through millennia of coevolution flowers became colorful; at the same time bees developed color vision, allowing them to spot flowers among the foliage. Unlike humans, bees are unreceptive to red, but they perceive ultraviolet as a distinct color, and some flowers we see as white appear as a vibrant ultraviolet color to bees. Thus, bees bypass red flowers and frequent blue, yellow, and white ones, especially when the latter appear to them as ultraviolet.

BUMBLEBEES AS POLLINATORS

Bumblebees exist on pollen and nectar, and their bodies have developed

structural adaptations to help gather this food. A coating of long, branched hairs accumulates pollen. Stiff hairs on the forelegs comb pollen from these hairs and pack it into hollowed out sections of the hind legs that serve as carrying baskets. Sharp spurs on the bee's middle legs pry the pollen masses loose back at the nest.

Some bumblebees have short tongues, whereas others have tongues that can measure an inch long. The long-tongued bumblebees are normally attracted to long corolla-tubed flowers where they collect nectar with their tongues, transfer the liquid to their honey stomachs, and then disgorge it into honey pots within their nests.

Elephanthead
Pedicularis groenlandica Retz.

Snapdragon Family
Scrophulariaceae

The long dense spikes of little pink flowers reward a close look. Each blossom resembles a miniature elephant's head, with two upper corolla lobes uniting to form the trunk, two side lobes forming the ears, and the smaller fifth lobe fitting under the trunk like a lower jaw. Unbranched stems are up to two feet tall. Lance-shaped leaves are mostly basal and so deeply incised as to appear fernlike. Blooming from June to August, these beauties frequent marshy ground in meadows and near streams and ponds from the ponderosa pine to the alpine zone.

Elephanthead Pollination

Elephantheads are nectarless, offering only pollen to their insect pollinators. Collecting pollen from the flower requires a learned behavior from a bumblebee of a precise size. The style, extending beyond the tip of the tube, is the first part of the flower to touch a visiting bee and receives the pollen brought by the bee from other elephanthead flowers. To gather pollen, bumblebees must complete an acrobatic exercise of pushing the tiny trunk upward with their head while pressing down the lower part of the flower with their hind legs. Then the bee vibrates its wings, forcing a small yellow cloud of pollen out of the anthers that is caught in the hairs of the bee's abdomen. Most of the pollen will be carried back to the hive for food, but some will remain on the bee to fertilize the next visited flower.

Elephanthead and Parasitism

Like Indian paintbrush, elephanthead is a partial root parasite. Only a portion of the food it requires is manufactured in its leaves; supplementary nutrients must be obtained from the roots of neighboring plants. Fleshy elephanthead roots taste like parsnips, but before sampling one, be sure to examine nearby plants. An elephanthead parasitizing the roots of a poisonous plant will accumulate toxic substances in its tissues.

How Elephanthead Was Named

The common name for elephanthead is, of course, self-evident. Elephanthead and its close relatives are named for the Latin word *pedicul*, meaning "louse." In English the name is lousewort, for it was thought that this plant increased the presence of lice in foraging cattle. Anders Retzius, the botanist who named this species, thought that it grew in Greenland, thus calling it *groenlandica*. He was wrong, but the name remains.

Scarlet Penstemon
Penstemon barbatus (Cav.) Roth

Snapdragon Family
Scrophulariaceae

Bright red flowers hang in loose clusters along one side of a tall upright stem. Each inch-long narrow tube gradually broadens toward the opening. The lower lobe bends back sharply and bears sparse golden hairs. Four stamens are enclosed in the upper lip; the fifth, which is sterile, lies along the throat. Five-inch narrow leaves are mostly basal. Blooming from midsummer into fall, scarlet penstemons are frequently spotted in dry open areas, but only in the southern part of our mountains, where they range from the ponderosa pine to the spruce-fir zone.

From a distance their crimson tubular flowers on tall stalks may be confused with scarlet gilia. The penstemon, however, has rounded corolla lobes and a bilaterally symmetrical shape, whereas scarlet gilia flowers are angular with five sharply pointed uniform lobes. Furthermore, penstemon leaves are opposite and entire; the gilia's are alternate and dissected.

COMMON NAMES
The advantages of common plant names include being part of the local vernacular as well as being easy to pronounce and spell, but they are not standardized as are Latin names. Scarlet penstemon, for example, also goes by the names of red penstemon, scarlet bugler, and hummingbird flower; the last name can be applied to most any red-flowered plant. Another name, golden beard, refers to the golden hairs inside the flower of this penstemon. In northern New Mexico and southern Colorado the Spanish name for the plant is *varita de San Jose*—"Saint Joseph's staff."

Hummingbird Magnets

Red flowers the size and shape of the birds' bill signal a source of nectar available to hummingbirds. Because they carry more pollen on their bodies than insects and disperse it over a greater area on their long flights than insects can, they are preferred pollinators. Hummingbirds have excellent color vision, a poor sense of smell, and a high metabolic rate requiring copious amounts of nectar. Thus, scarlet penstemon and other flowers that attract hummingbird pollinators are brightly colored, odorless, and produce nectar in abundance.

The late-summer flowering of scarlet penstemon and other red flowers coincides with Rufous Hummingbird migration southward along the Southern Rockies. Each tiny Rufous must regularly interrupt its long journey with respites

of a few days in mountain meadows to replenish energy. Flitting from flower to flower, it sucks up nectar through a long hollow tongue. Then, with a full stomach it perches on an open branch to digest the meal, all the while mindful of protecting its territory. Any other hummingbird that intrudes is forcefully driven off. With strength restored, the hummer continues on its journey until it needs to feed again. This territorial habit is apparent at home bird feeders, where Rufous individuals shoo away all other hummingbirds.

Dusky Penstemon
Penstemon whippleanus Gray

Snapdragon Family
Scrophulariaceae

Drooping inch-long flowers cluster along the upper part of eighteen-inch erect stems. The plump blooms are usually dark purple, but wine-red, even cream-colored, forms occur. The lower lip projects beyond the upper, and the slightly spreading lobes bear long white hairs. Dark green oval leaves may be lightly toothed along the edges; stem leaves are opposite. Stems, leaves, and flowers are hairy. Dusky penstemon blooms in June and July in meadows and exposed rocky sites in the Douglas-fir and spruce-fir vegetation zones.

BEARDTONGUES

Look inside the throat of a penstemon flower, and you will find an enlarged sterile stamen lying atop the lower lip. Because in most species it is hairy, one of the common names for penstemon is beardtongue. Whereas the typical Snapdragon Family flower has four stamens that curve to fit inside the upper lip, this genus, with its additional sterile stamen, is appropriately named *Penstemon*, meaning "five stamens." The fifth fills the flower opening like a bearded tongue. The hairs prevent small insects from entering, provide a foothold for bees, and reduce nectar evaporation. Yet dusky penstemon is an exception, for its "tongue" is beardless.

PENSTEMON POLLINATION

Most penstemons are pollinated by bees that land on the lower lip where visual and scent cues direct them to the nectar at the back of the flower. As they proceed to their sugary meal, their weight causes the four fertile stamens to spring down from above and apply pollen to the upper body of the bee. Some bees with short tongues discover how to reach the nectaries in long corolla-tubed penstemons simply by crawling to the base of the tube, where they cut a circular hole in the flower. They then extend their tongues through the hole and lap up the nectar without ever crawling into the mouth of the corolla.

ROBBERS AND THIEVES

Insects guilty of breaking and entering by damaging a flower to steal nectar without

performing a service of pollination in return are termed nectar robbers. Penstemon flowers are vulnerable to nectar robbers and also to another form of nectar loss. Nectar thieves are little insects that crawl into a flower, drink the nectar, and then leave but are too small to be pollinators. With a "bearded tongue" at the flower entrance, penstemons are able to protect themselves from nectar thieves, because small insects cannot penetrate the tangled hairs.

Twinflower
Linnaea borealis L.

Honeysuckle Family
Caprifoliaceae

Pairs of dainty, pink bell-shaped flowers dangle from the forked tops of three-inch-tall flowering stalks. The half-inch-long flowers exude a pleasing fragrance. Leaves of this matted, creeping plant are oval with a few teeth toward the tip. Twinflower is a common ground cover in deep Douglas-fir and spruce-fir forests but is often overlooked when not in bloom.

The genus is named for Carl Linnaeus, who considered twinflower his favorite plant, and portraits show the great botanist holding a sprig of it. He wrote that the plant was "lowly, insignificant, flowering but for a brief space, [like] Linnaeus, who resembles it."

CARL LINNAEUS (1707–1778)
Modern botany had its beginnings with this Swedish physician who had an early intense interest in plants. In his youth he held positions at various European botanical gardens, writing scientific papers and meeting prominent botanists. At the age of twenty-eight he received his degree in medicine—appropriately, as botany

and medicine were closely entwined. The same year saw the publication of his landmark treatise, *Systema Naturae*, a hierarchical classification of the natural world. Throughout his life he published new and ever-expanding editions.

Linnaeus helped found the Royal Swedish Academy of Sciences. He became the personal physician to the Swedish royal family, was granted nobility, and by the end of his career was famous worldwide. But his success required so much public involvement that he eventually had little time for active botany. He wrote to a colleague, "Once I had plants and no money. Now, what is money good for, without plants?"

HONEYSUCKLE FAMILY

Principally a family of shrubs and small trees, the Honeysuckle Family is characterized by its simple and opposite leaves. The flowers, which are usually in pairs, consist of five petals joined together. Snowberries, honeysuckles, and viburnum are important cultivars.

Red Elderberry

Sambucus racemosa L.

Honeysuckle Family
Caprifoliaceae

In the fall clusters of bright red berries contrast with shiny green leaves on up to ten-foot-tall elderberry shrubs. Earlier in the season tiny white saucer-shaped flowers bloom in pyramidal clusters that may be six inches wide. The opposite leaves are compound with seven coarsely toothed leaflets that are pointed at the tip and lopsided at the base. Elderberries are common in moist clearings and along streams in the Douglas-fir and spruce-fir vegetation zones.

USES OF ELDERBERRY

Elderberry wood is hard—ideal for cabinetry—but because of the trunk's limited size, it has been used mostly for carving toys. Flutes and whistles are easily made by removing the pith from stems. Elderberry also occurs in Europe, where it is represented in mythology and history; in fact, the name *Sambucus* is derived from the Greek word *sambuca*—a stringed musical instrument made from this shrub. In northern New Mexico and southern Colorado Hispanics call this plant *flor de sauz* or willow flower, for the willow shape of the leaflets. Wine and jelly are made from blue-berried species of elderberry, but cyanide-producing glycosides render the red berries of their species toxic.

Compound Leaves

Leaves may be simple, with one blade, or compound, with more than one leaflet like elderberry. For plant identification it is important to know whether you are looking at one small leaf or a large leaf composed of smaller leaflets. The clue to determining the kind of leaf is a tiny bud at the attachment of leaf to stem. Where the leaflets attach, there is no bud.

The arrangement of leaflets may be radiating from a single point at the tip of the stem or lined up along the stem in pairs. Radiating leaflets are termed palmate, like fingers spreading from a palm. The term for leaflets paired along the stem is pinnate, from the Greek word for "feather."

Harebell
Campanula rotundifolia L.

Harebell Family
Campanulaceae

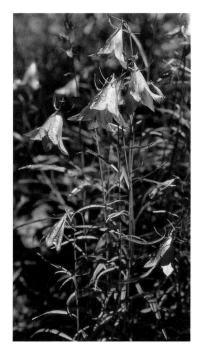

Round blue bells dangle from two-foot slender stalks. The inch-long corolla has five pointed, curved lobes. Narrow stem-leaves are three inches long. Spreading by means of underground stems, harebell can aggressively colonize meadows and mountain slopes from the ponderosa pine to the alpine vegetation zone.

Linnaeus named the genus *Campanula*, meaning "little bell." He gave this plant a specific epithet that translates to "round leaves," seemingly a misnomer, considering that the stem leaves are linear on mature plants. Though round leaves won't be visible on mature harebells in the field, the first pair to emerge on these plants is actually round. Overseas this circumboreal species is the "bluebells of Scotland." Parry's harebell (*Campanula parryi*), a closely related species, occurs in damp meadows at high elevations. These plants are shorter, with a single flower on each stem, and all leaves are linear, including the basal ones. In contrast to the nodding flowers of the common harebell, upright purple ones face the sky with their spreading corolla lobes.

Harebell Family

Harebell Family leaves are alternate and simple; the flowers have five joined petals and five stamens. Self-fertilization is prevented by the growth sequence of the sexual organs, where anthers mature before the pistil, and pollen is carried away by insects. After several days the pollen is gone, and the flower becomes receptive to pollen brought in from other flowers. Lobelia is an attractive and easy-to-grow ornamental, as are numerous *Campanula* cultivars, collectively known as bellflowers.

LINNEAUS'S BINOMIAL SYSTEM

Linnaeus assigned a unique double name to every plant and animal. The first word is the genus—a small group of similar organisms to which the plant or animal belongs. The second, the specific epithet, distinguishes individual species from others of the same genus. Because Latin was the language of science in

the eighteenth century, binomials are in Latin form and always italicized, and the genus is capitalized. Biologists everywhere in the world communicate with this universal system, and every newly discovered living thing, from bacteria to primates, is named according to his binomial rule. Without doubt, Linneaus is the Father of Modern Botany.

Northern Bedstraw
Galium boreale L.

Madder Family
Rubiaceae

Thick sprays of petite white flowers are clustered atop leafy stems that may reach two feet tall. The fragrant flowers have four spreading pointed lobes and four stamens. Smooth leaves are long and narrow with three prominent veins. Leaves in whorls of four on a succulent square stem are a distinctive feature of northern bedstraw. It blooms throughout the summer from the piñon-juniper to the spruce-fir vegetation zone.

Cleavers (*Galium aparine*) is a related, less common species introduced from Europe. Its weak stems form vinelike mats over and through taller herbs and shrubs. This straggly species differs from northern bedstraw by its stiff, hooked hairs that feel rough to the touch and by its leaves that grow in whorls of six rather than four.

MADDER FAMILY

This is a large family of tropical trees and shrubs, with *Galium* the only genus occurring in the Southern Rockies. *Rubiaceae* is from the Greek word for "red," and *Galium* is Greek for "milk," for some species were used in the past to curdle milk. *Boreale* means "northern."

Economic Uses

Two Madder Family species have provided highly valued commodities—one during ancient times, the other cherished more than ever today. The roots of madder (*Rubia tinctoria*) were used to produce red dye for at least 5,000 years in the Old World, and madder was continuously grown as a major crop until synthetic dyes appeared in the early 1800s. An Ethiopian native coffee (*Caffea arabica*) is the source of the popular stimulant, caffeine.

In addition, the bark of the cinchona tree yields the drug quinine, until recently the most

effective treatment for malaria. Cleavers, with its sticky stem and leaf hairs that prevent the plants from packing down, has been employed as mattress filling, and bedstraw was once fed to geese, giving it the alternative name goosegrass. Dried and roasted seeds of cleavers are still used as a coffee substitute in Ireland.

Yarrow
Achillea millefolium L.

Aster Family
Asteraceae

Flat-topped clusters of white flowers sit on upright, two-foot-tall stems. Each bundle is composed of numerous tiny flower heads that have three to six broad rays surrounding a dozen or more tan disk flowers. The rays are usually white but may be pink at higher elevations. Dense silky hairs covering the stems and finely divided leaves cast a gray tone to the plant. The entire plant exudes a pungent odor. Blooming all season long, colonies of yarrow are found at every elevation in the Southern Rockies except on the highest summits.

Because of its clusters of small flower heads and dissected leaves, yarrow is often confused with Carrot Family plants. But close observation reveals that yarrow flowers are arranged in composite heads with disk and ray flowers characteristic of the Aster Family. Furthermore, yarrow leaves are not stem claspers like those of members of the Carrot Family. When out of bloom, yarrow, with its dissected leaves, could be mistaken for a fern were it not for the strong aroma imparted by volatile foliage oils.

YARROW'S NAMES

According to tradition, this plant takes its name after Achilles, who used the plant to staunch the flow of blood from his wounded soldiers during the Trojan War. Yarrow sap, with its high tannin content, has been used by armies in such a way since antiquity, gaining it the name *herbal militaris*. *Millefolium* means "thousand leaves," referring to the many lobes on each leaf. The local Spanish name, *plumajillo*, or little feather, also relates to these leaves.

Medicinal Properties

Native Americans and early settlers used yarrow for its astringent qualities—those that made it effective for Achilles' men. When England experienced a pharmaceutical drug shortage during World War II, the Ministry of Health recruited boy scouts, girl guides, and schoolchildren to scour the countryside for yarrow to augment supplies. Because of its healing qualities, herbal teas made from yarrow are available in health food stores throughout the United States and Europe.

Even today, yarrow is yielding new medicinal rewards. Swedish scientists have found that yarrow tissues contain mosquito-repellent compounds. When volunteers placed their hands into cages containing *Aedes egyptii* mosquitoes, which are transmitters of yellow fever and other tropical diseases, the mosquitoes avoided hands treated with *Achillea* extract. Separating and identifying the repellent compounds may lead to an important tool in controlling mosquito-borne diseases.

Pearly Everlasting
Anaphalis margaritacea (L.) Benth.

Aster Family
Asteraceae

Clusters of round flower heads top foot-tall erect stems. White papery bracts enclose each head like a pearl. As heads mature, the bracts fold back, revealing yellow disk flowers. Three-inch-long lance-shaped leaves are green above and covered with white woolly hairs beneath. Unbranched stems, also covered with matted woolly hairs, spread by extensive underground stems called rhizomes. Blooming in late summer, patches of pearly everlasting frequent roadsides and other open areas from the ponderosa pine zone to timberline.

RELATED PLANTS

Also common in our region, pussytoes (*Antennaria* spp.) are smaller plants growing in extensive mats of basal leaves. Their soft, fuzzy, pink or white floral heads do, indeed, resemble furry pussy toes. Hybridization is common in this genus, making species delineation difficult. A greater challenge for botanists is that nearly all plants are female, and, therefore, reproduction results in clones.

NAME AUTHORITY

The Latin name for each plant is followed by the abbreviation of the name of the person who initially applied that name to the plant. In this case the "(L.)" after *Anaphalis margaritacea* means that Carl Linneaus

applied the specific epithet, *margaritacea*, meaning "pearl." The parentheses around the L. indicate that the plant was later found to belong in a different genus. The name following (L.) signifies that George Bentham assigned the species to the genus *Anaphalis* but retained the specific epithet.

Uses of Pearly Everlasting

Cut plants maintain a pleasant fragrance for many months and were used by the colonists to freshen clothes closets and by Indians in the Northwest to sweeten baby cradles. The dried stalks with their pearly white heads are favorite additions to floral arrangements.

Mountain Thistle

Cirsium eatonii (Gray) Robins.

Up to three feet tall, this massive plant stands out for its pale, woolly appearance. Flower heads are congested in a heavy, nodding bunch at the top of each stem. Dense clusters of pale heads, each composed of tightly packed white to yellow florets, are protected within long, spiny bracts and leaves. Masses of white hairs among the spines convey a cobwebby appearance. Insulated by this hairy covering, mountain thistle thrives on cold high rocky slopes in the spruce-fir and alpine zones.

Cirsium is the ancient Greek word for "swollen vein," referring to the plant's purported ability to cure such a problem.
Thistle is from the Old English *thistel*, meaning "sharp."

THE GENUS CIRSIUM

Thistles are easily recognized, for they are the only plants in the Southern Rockies having leaves covered with long spines. Powder puff flower heads are composed of dozens of long, narrow disk flowers; ray flowers are lacking. Several species inhabit our region, among them the stemless meadow thistle (*Cirsium scariosum*), which consists merely of a basal rosette of spiny leaves with flower heads in the center. The common elk thistle (*C. foliosum*), with white to purple flowers and stems that are thick and succulent from bottom to top, is restricted to wet mountain meadows and riparian habitats.

Despite the spines, thistle parts are edible and can be added to salads or cooked. Fleshy taproots, basal leaves, and young flower stalks are collected between fall and early spring. Goldfinches nest in mid-July when thistle flower heads are maturing. They perch on top of the heads, pecking to gather the fluffy seeds, and then, with beaks filled with fluff, fly off to build their nests.

Weedy Thistles

With a long history in North America, Canada thistle (*Cirsium arvense*) is all too common. French settlers unwittingly brought it to Canada in contaminated crop seeds in the seventeenth century, and by 1795 Vermont had to enact legislation to control this pest. Emerging from rapidly spreading underground stems and producing new flower stalks each year, it is one of our most pernicious weeds and is extremely difficult to extirpate from croplands. Although other noxious weeds can be controlled by plowing under before flowering, that technique cuts Canada thistle roots into parts, and each piece sprouts a new stem. It's also a pasture nuisance, because the spines render it useless for forage.

Biological control—using imported organisms to control pests—was tried on another troublesome introduced species, the musk thistle (*Carduus nutans*). Eurasian weevils released into

infected fields burrow into musk thistle flower heads and devour their seeds. The project was successful, saving farmers millions in reduced herbicide costs. Only after the weevils became established was it discovered that they also feed on native thistles, including endangered species. So now the weevils themselves must be controlled.

Showy Daisy
Erigeron speciosus (Lindl.) DC

Aster Family
Asteraceae

These pale pink to lavender daisies have inch-wide flower heads with dozens of long narrow ray petals surrounding a yellow quarter-inch-wide disk. Bracts beneath each flower head are hairy, and all are of equal length. The bases of the lancelike leaves clasp the stem. This abundant wildflower brightens open forest landscapes in the piñon-juniper, ponderosa pine, and Douglas-fir zones during most of the growing season.

SHOWY DAISY NAMES

Ancient Greeks first applied the name *Erigeron*, meaning "old man," because, after flowering, the head is covered with feathery white bristles resembling an old man's hair. Plants in this huge genus are called fleabanes. The suffix *bane* means "deadly" or "poison," suggesting that these plants are repellent to fleas. *Daisy* was first applied to a small pink and white English daisy that closes at nightfall and opens again at sunrise. Thus it is the eye of the day, or "day's eye."

ASTER FAMILY

The trend from large single flowers to clusters of smaller ones is evident during the 120 million years of flowering plant evolution, with the Aster Family achieving the ultimate condition in this line of development. In this family what appears to be a single flower is a flower head composed of many undersized flowers in a dense cluster.

This is also known as the Composite Family, because each "flower" is actually a composite of many small specialized flowers, or florets. A series of modified leaves, or bracts, at the base of the flower head forms an involucre that, like sepals in other families, protects young flowers in bud and protects mature heads from plant-eating insects.

Yet another common name is Sunflower Family, and, using an analogy to the sun, the center of the floral head is termed the "disk," and the long petals on the edge, the "rays." The disk consists of numerous florets that, despite their small size, have normal petals, stamens, and pistils and produce one seed. Each ray floret has a single colorful strap-shaped petal that enhances the visibility of the flower head to foraging insects. Within the family are many variations on this theme. Flower heads may consist of only disk florets, or only ray florets, or, more commonly, both. Ray and disk florets may be few or many, large or small.

Not only have plants in the Aster Family evolved radical changes in floral structure, they also have developed more effective compounds to deter herbivores. Indeed, the success of this family—today one of the largest—is attributed as much to the increasing variety of these new compounds as to the innovation of floral structures.

Showy Goldeneye
Heliomeris multiflora Nutt.

Aster Family

Asteraceae

These three-foot-tall branching plants have many sunflowerlike floral heads on wiry stems. A dozen or so yellow rays surround the golden disk flowers; involucral bracts covered with stiff hairs are narrow, unequal in length, and arranged in two rows. Rough lance-shaped leaves are three inches long, with the lower ones paired. Flowering from summer to late fall, showy goldeneye is common on dry slopes and along highways at all elevations below the alpine vegetation zone.

HOW BOTANISTS NAME PLANTS

When a plant is discovered that is new to science, a botanist assigns it a Latinized two-part name. The first word of this binomial is the genus, designating the group of closely related plants to which it belongs. The second—in this case *multiflora*, meaning "many flowered"—is the specific epithet that distinguishes this plant from the others of its genus.

To be accepted by the scientific community, the name must be published with a detailed description of the new plant in Latin, including an explanation of how the plant differs from closely related plants along with data on where and when the plant was collected. A specimen must be preserved, and its place of deposition must be included in the published account.

Most wildflower enthusiasts refer to plants by their common names, and botanists often do so informally. Common names are in the local vernacular, their meaning is apparent, and laypersons can pronounce them. Nevertheless,

lack of specificity can be a problem because common names often vary geographically. They may refer to more than one kind of plant (for example, goldeneye is sometimes applied to *Heterotheca* ssp., another common genus in the Southern Rockies), or one plant may have more than one name. Scientists rely on Latin plant names because each uniquely refers to a single species, and they are universally understood.

Orange Sneezeweed

Aster Family

Hymenoxys hoopesii (Gray) Bierner

Asteraceae

Coarse, leafy two-foot stems bear large sunflowerlike flower heads. Numerous inch-long yellow-orange rays notched at the tip surround a flat disk of purple florets in early summer. Later the disk becomes yellow and convex, and the rays droop. The two rows of flower bracts are narrow with tips bending out and down. Alternate leaves may be a foot long at the base but are progressively smaller up the stem. Broad patches of sneezeweed create golden fields in moist meadows from the ponderosa pine to the spruce-fir vegetation zone.

Other plants in the Southern Rockies with large sunflowerlike flower heads and large leaves are mulesears (*Wyethia amplexicaulis*), a low plant with basal leaves; balsamroot (*Balsamorhiza sagittata*), over two feet tall with silvery, arrow-shaped leaves; and nodding sunflower (*Helianthella quinquenervis*), a four- to five-foot-tall erect plant. All but nodding sunflower have thick taproots that were used medicinally by Native Americans.

Sneezeweed is toxic to sheep, causing them to come down with spewing sickness; however, cattle rarely eat the plant. Sneezeweed provided Navajos with medicine and chewing gum as well as a yellow dye.

Changing Names

Older botanical guides refer to this plant as *Helenium hoopesii* or *Dugaldia hoopesii*, but recent biochemical and chromosomal data make clear that this species is most closely related to plants in the *Hymenoxys* genus. Despite the fact that botanists have moved sneezeweed around from one genus to another, the specific epithet, *hoopesii*, remains the same. The name given to a species when it is first described stays with the plant no matter how many times it is placed in a different genus. *Hoopesii* honors Thomas Hoopes, a prospector who accompanied a topographic survey for railroad routes in Colorado in 1861 when orange sneezeweed was first discovered.

It is pure coincidence that *hoopesii* sounds like a sneeze, though with its disheveled rays the flower does look as if it might have just sneezed. The flower's name most likely derives from the use of the powdered leaves for snuff.

Nodding Groundsel
Senecio bigelovii Gray

Rayless cylindrical flower heads droop from up to three-foot-tall, erect leafy stems. Twenty or so long, narrow involucral bracts envelope the cylindrical head, below which is an additional set of four to ten sharply pointed bracts. Lance-shaped leaves four to eight inches long have teeth along the edges. Blooming from July to September, nodding groundsel is common in damp meadows in the Douglas-fir and spruce-fir vegetation zones. It rarely occurs in the Colorado Front Range, however.

A Huge Genus

Senecio, one of the largest genera of flowering plants, with over 1,000 species worldwide, includes annuals, perennials, and shrubs. Yellow flower heads with involucral bracts of equal length like a miniature picket fence, above another series of a few shorter bracts, characterize the American members of this genus. Its name derives from the Latin root for "old man," referring to the long, soft white bristles remaining after flowering that resemble hair on the heads of some elderly men. But that feature is hardly unique among Aster Family plants; for example, see showy daisy (p. 128–129).

Dozens of species are native to our area, most with yellow ray flowers. *Senecio bigelovii* was originally described from a specimen collected in New Mexico's Sandia Mountains in the early 1850s by John Bigelow, the surgeon-botanist on the Pacific Rail Survey that traveled along the thirty-fifth parallel.

INSECT POLLINATION

A variety of insects pollinate nodding groundsel floral heads. Flies, beetles, and other short-tongue insects collect the pollen that lies upon the reduced flower surface; butterflies and moths, with their much longer tongues, extract the nectar from the base of the disk flowers.

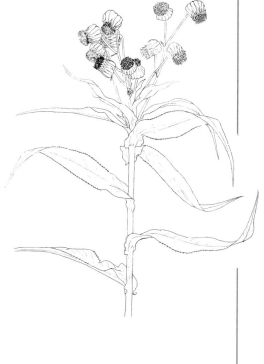

The Wildflowers 🌿 135

Nodding Onion
Allium cernuum Roth

Dainty pink flowers on long stems radiate from the tip of a foot-tall stalk like points of light in a starburst. Stalks bearing a dozen or more bell-like flowers in an umbel bend over near the top and resemble a miniature shepherd's crook. Three to six slender leaves at the base of each plant emit an oniony odor when bruised. Nodding onion is commonly found on grassy slopes and in dry meadows from the ponderosa pine to the spruce-fir vegetation zone.

Several other native wild onion species inhabit our area; however, their pink or white umbel flower clusters face upward from straight stalks.

A Related Onion

Geyer onion (*A. geyeri*), an inhabitant of the higher moisture areas, shares the umbel arrangement of flowers with nodding onion, but the stem is straight and the flowers face the sky. Instead of umbels of flowers, some Geyer onion plants have umbels of bulblets, smooth, shiny red bulbs, sometimes with slender leaves. These plants reproduce not by seeds but by these small bulbs that fall to the ground and start a new plant. Bulblets fall farther from the parent plant than seeds and have a higher survival rate. Because they are not formed from fertilization, their genetic makeup is identical to the mother plant's.

Lily Family

Plants in the Lily Family produce flowers with three sepals and three petals that are usually alike in color and size. Leaf veins are parallel.

Plants are perennial, arising from bulbs, rhizomes, corms, or tubers. Edible members include asparagus, onion, garlic, and leek; hyacinth, tulip, lily-of-the-valley, and fritillaria are among the ornamentals.

CULTIVATED ALLIUMS

Three species—common onion, garlic, and leek—were cultivated in Egypt some 5,000 years ago. Columbus brought cultivated onion and leek bulbs to America on his second voyage, and garlic followed shortly afterward. Chives and shallots, likewise initially domesticated from Old World species, are also *Allium* cultivars.

ONION FLAVOR

Volatile sulfur compounds in all parts of the plant give onions the piquancy so appreciated by humans. With their high vitamin C content, wild onions were one of the few plants to provide a combination of nutrition and seasoning to the diets of virtually all American Indians. The plants are relished by wildlife, but when cows eat onions, their milk becomes tainted.

During the Lewis and Clark Expedition, Meriwether Lewis proclaimed the nodding onion to be valuable "inasmuch as it produces a large quantity to the squar [*sic*] foot and bears with ease the rigor of this climate, and withal I think it as pleasantly flavored as any species of the root I ever tasted."

Gunnison's Mariposa Lily

Calochortus gunnisonii S. Wats.

Lily Family

Liliaceae

Single tuliplike flowers on foot-tall bare stems have three large white or purple petals that are marked at the base with ornate patches of yellow hairs bordered by purple. Narrow similarly marked sepals are barely visible between the petals. Mariposa lilies seem to be almost all stem and flower, though a few long narrow leaves arise from the base of each plant. Blooming in early summer in grassy meadows and clearings, this species has adapted to a wide range of elevations—from piñon-juniper to the alpine zone.

WIDESPREAD IN THE WEST

Of the sixty or so species of *Calochortus*, the greatest diversity is found in California, with a few found along the coast from British Columbia to Guatemala and inland to Kansas. Two are native to the Southern Rockies. This distribution pattern indicates that the genus originated and diverged into species in California, and then a few species spread farther afield.

White, pink, lemon yellow, orange, crimson, purple, and even brown or bluish hues embellish the flowers of these plants, and many display blossoms mottled with spectacular intricate inner petal markings. Several species are propagated for use in rock gardens and as border plants.

Appropriate Nomenclature

The name for the genus is on-target, since *Calochortus* is Greek for "beautiful grass," and the plants do resemble grasses before they bloom. *Mariposa* means "butterfly" in Spanish, for the delicate colorful petals fluttering in the wind.

John Williams Gunnison (1812–1853)

John Gunnison, a military engineer assigned to a survey team looking for potential routes for a rail line to the Pacific, collected plants along the way. His party was massacred by Indians when it reached an encampment in Utah. The city of Gunnison, Colorado, and a major river famous for its fly-fishing are named after him.

Indian and Settler Food

The thick-scaled bulb, about six inches below ground surface, nourished Indians and settlers alike. Indians gathered the bulbs in spring before the plants flowered, eating them raw or baked. For a few weeks in 1848 bulbs of a related species, the sego lily, kept Mormon settlers from starving when their crops were decimated by locusts. In commemoration, the sego lily is now Utah's state flower.

Fawn Lily
Erythronium grandiflorum Pursh

Lily Family
Liliaceae

Two-inch spherical yellow flowers dangle from leafless stalks. Six yellow petals and sepals curve gracefully backward, and the stamens hang straight down. Two smooth bright green elliptical leaves emerge from the base of each ten-inch leafless stalk. Extensive patches of fawn lilies transform open meadows and streamsides into fields of yellow as mountain snows recede—in early April at lower elevations but not until midsummer in the spruce-fir and alpine zones.

A Plethora of Names

Such a lovely plant has long attracted attention, as reflected by the plethora of names attributed to it. Avalanche lily, snow lily, and glacier lily are names that refer to its habit of blooming within sight of melting snow. Trout lily is heard in the eastern United States, because its leaves are mottled with brown splotches similar to the lateral markings on an eastern brook trout. Another name, adder's tongue, describes the shape of either the protruding stamens or the sharp points of the plant's emerging leaves. Strangely enough, dogtooth violet is yet another appellation, though this plant hasn't the slightest resemblance to a violet. The underground bulb of a closely related European species is white and shaped like a dog's tooth, however. Fawn lily most likely refers to the paired leaves resembling the ears of a fawn; in fact, the celebrated early American naturalist John Burroughs wrote, "Two leaves stand up like fawn's ears, and this feature with its recurved petals, gives it a wide-awake look."

When Linnaeus named the genus *Erythronium*, derived from a Greek word meaning "red," the lone species in this genus known at the time had red flowers. That name persists, notwithstanding the addition of fawn lily and numerous other non-red species to the genus.

ANCIENT ROOT USES

Embedded deeply underground, fawn lily bulbs have long provided an important source of food for natives inhabiting the Pacific Northwest. Archaeological evidence suggests that lily bulbs were steam roasted in 3,000-year-old roasting pits excavated in British Columbia. Indications are that the roots were collected, stored, and traded in large quantities and that those early people not only developed an ecological understanding of the species but also practiced management strategies for assuring a constant supply. Thompson River and other Indians in the Northwest still steam roast the mild sweet bulbs in pits for as long as thirty-six hours and then add them to stews, soups, or puddings.

FOOD FOR GRIZZLIES

After observing bears returning to the same locations year after year to dig for fawn lily bulbs, research naturalists in Glacier National Park discovered that the act of churning the ground results in significantly more available nitrogen in the soil. It turns out that lilies in these preferred sites are more nutritious and produce more seeds—an example of a mutually beneficial relationship between bear and plant.

Star Solomon's Seal
Maianthemum stellatum (L.) Link

Lily Family
Liliaceae

Arching leafy stems up to three feet long terminate in a loose cluster of a dozen dainty white flowers resembling miniature six-pointed stars. Lance-shaped strongly veined leaves attach directly to the stem in zigzag fashion. Star Solomon's seal blooms early in the season; by summer black- and red-striped berries replace the blossoms. Covering the ground in deep moist woods from the ponderosa pine to the spruce-fir zone, star Solomon's seal is a common late-spring treasure.

A Close Relative

False Solomon's seal (*Maianthemum racemosum*) has larger, broader (half as wide as long) leaves with lobes at the base that partially enclose the stem. The flowers are tinier and more numerous, with stamens protruding beyond the petals. The berries at maturity are red and usually wrinkled. The two species of Solomon's seal occasionally grow side by side.

Other Names

In older plant guides you will see star Solomon's seal and false Solomon's seal placed in the genus *Smilacina*. But now botanists have concluded that, on the basis of growth form, floral parts, and chromosome number, these species belong in the genus *Maianthemum*, a group popularly known as false lily-of-the-valley.

The origin of the name Solomon's seal is somewhat obscure. According to the *Oxford English Dictionary*, "The name has been variously explained as referring to the markings seen on a transverse section of the root-stock, or to the round scars left on this by the decay of the stems, or to the use of the root to seal and close up green wounds." *Maianthemum* means "May flower."

EDIBLE SOLOMON'S SEAL

The bittersweet berries are edible either raw or cooked, and young shoots can be used for potherbs. Although many Native Americans collected Solomon's seal berries for a summer diet supplement, the principal indigenous use of both species throughout North America has been for medicine.

EARTH PLANTS

Ecologists categorize Solomon's seals as geophytes, a word coined from the Greek roots for "earth plants." Geophytes live on the floor of heavily canopied forests, but, whereas their shade-tolerant neighbors manufacture food from filtered sunlight, earth plants can only capture energy from direct sunlight. They emerge in early spring before trees leaf out and in only a matter of weeks set seeds, at the same time generating a year's supply of food that is root stored. Their showy flowers must compete for the pollination services of those few insects active so early in the year. By the time the forest floor becomes shaded, geophytes wither and, for the remainder of the year, persist totally underground in the form of starchy tubers.

Death Camas

Zigadenus elegans Pursh

A long loose cluster of white flowers tops a two-foot-tall leafless stem. The half-inch-wide saucer-shaped flowers have three sepals and three petals that look identical (each with a green tinge at the base) and six stamens. Flowers are nodding in bud and erect when open. The foot-long, narrow basal leaves display prominent veins. Death camas blooms in summer along streamsides and in moist meadows from the ponderosa pine to the spruce-fir zone.

Zigadenus means "yoke glands," referring to the pair of glands at the base of each flower segment. This is the original spelling of the word, coined by the botanist who described the first species. Frequently you see the name spelled *Zygadenus*, a more faithful transcription of the Greek root, but the original spelling is correct under the rules of botanical nomenclature.

A Deadly Plant

Death camas tissues contain toxic alkaloids. Unfortunately, before blooming it resembles edible relatives such as wild onion, quamash, and mariposa lilies—so much so that Indians and early settlers sometimes mistakenly ate the bulbs with disastrous results. Today an emergency room still occasionally receives a vomiting patient who has been poisoned by ingesting death camas.

The poisonous alkaloids that protect the plant from herbivores are in the nectar, as well. Nectar that is toxic to insects would seem

counterproductive; however, some insects—
the ones that pollinate death camas—are
resistant to the poison. Those lethally affected
are small insects that try to steal the nectar
without carrying away pollen. People who manage
honeybee colonies must be aware of where their
bees forage, for humans can be poisoned from death
camas–contaminated honey.

Wand lily, another common name, describes
the erect flowering stem bearing the long white flower
cluster. Such a magnificent show will enhance any
garden, but you won't find death camas in a Canadian
garden. Because of the danger to livestock, the Canadian
government lists this species as a prohibited noxious weed, making it
illegal to import the seeds into the country.

MONOCOTS

The Lily Family belongs to a
division of flowering plants known
as monocots—a group that includes
lilies, grasses, orchids, and a few
other lesser families. Monocot
wildflowers are easy to recognize
because the number of sepals,
petals, stamens, and stigmas is
always divisible by three. Also, leaf
veins are parallel instead of in a
network. Monocot seedlings bear
a single initial leaf, or cotyledon;
all other flowering plant seedlings
have two cotyledons and, thus, are
known as dicots.

Rocky Mountain Iris
Iris missouriensis Nutt.

Iris Family
Iridaceae

Wild irises are fully as showy and complex as their horticultural relatives. Three pale blue petals are erect; the three broad sepals with darker veins hang down. A flat style branch and one stamen lie above each sepal. Leafless stems reach two feet, and the flat, lance-shaped leaves are nearly as tall. Look for clumps of iris growing in moist meadows and along streamsides from the ponderosa pine up to the spruce-fir vegetation zone.

IRIS FAMILY

With three petals and three sepals, the flowers are similar to those of the Lily Family, but they differ in having three, rather than six, stamens. Long narrow leaves that fold at the center are characteristic of Iris Family plants. Each leaf enfolds younger leaves in an arrangement that Linnaeus termed "equitant"—meaning "riding horseback"—because one leaf seems astride the next. Ornamentals include gladiolus, crocus, freesia, and, above all, iris, with its thousands of named varieties and hybrids.

ECONOMIC USES OF FAMILY MEMBERS

Dried iris rootstocks yield orris, a violet-scented powder used in perfumery. Since the Middle Ages, when *orris* was a household word, its curative use has continued, particularly in the Orient to this day. Terpenes extracted from iris roots possess anticancer properties, but the root can be lethal if ingested. In fact, Indians dipped arrow points in a solution of ground root to poison enemy warriors.

Saffron, undoubtedly the world's most expensive spice, has been collected from the dried stigmas of a cultivated Old World crocus for at least four thousand years. The aromatic ambrosial yellow powder is used in fine cuisine, most notably the Spanish dish paella, and was used to dye the robes of Buddhist monks.

Although black bears find wild iris leaves edible, cattle avoid them, and increasing stands of iris may indicate overgrazing. When nearby vegetation is weakened by grazing, the robust, creeping underground iris rootstocks can withstand trampling and will spread.

IRIS IN HISTORY

The iris emblem on royal scepters has traditionally symbolized power, with the three parts of the flower representing wisdom, faith, and courage. Ever since King Louis VII of France selected the iris as his emblem, it has been known as *fleur-de-lis*, a corruption of *fleur-de-Louis*. *Iris*, the ancient Greek word for "rainbow," alludes to the colorful hues of the various species.

Rocky Mountain iris carries the name *missouriensis*, commemorating the locality of the first specimen collected near the headwaters of the Missouri River in 1834 by Nathaniel Wyeth, a Boston fur trader.

BEES AND IRIS FLOWERS

Iris flowers are exquisitely designed for bumblebee pollination. A bee lands on the drooping surface of one of the showy sepals and follows the dark blue lines that lead to the nectar source. It squeezes under the style, where pollen is scraped off the insect's back; then, after the bee is finished imbibing nectar, pollen is smeared onto its back as it exits.

Fairy Slipper

Calypso bulbosa (L.) Oakes

Orchid Family
Orchidaceae

You have to go on hands and knees to appreciate this exquisite jewel. Each dainty pastel pink and purple flower nods on a bare, four-inch-tall stalk. The three sepals and two upper petals are erect, pink, and narrow, with pointed tips; the large lower petal is a white spoon-shaped structure embellished with reddish purple spots and stripes and bearded with long yellow hairs. Patches of fairy slippers bloom as soon as ground is exposed from melting snow, but after flowering, the plants lose their above-ground parts, leaving only the underground bulbous root system and a single oval leaf to overwinter beneath the snow. Look for these diminutive plants on forest litter in the Douglas-fir and spruce-fir vegetation zones.

Calypso is named for the lovely nymph who waylaid Ulysses on his return to Ithaca after the Trojan War. For stunning beauty, few wildflowers encountered in the mountains of the West can rival it; consequently the species is now at risk. No wonder. A century ago a visitor to the grand hotel in Banff National Park noted that freshly picked fairy slippers decorated every dining room table, and that probably was common practice elsewhere. Fortunately, today most of us prefer to enjoy such magnificent flowers live in their natural habitat rather than in a vase.

A Deceptive Flower

A supreme moment in John Muir's life was when he discovered a calypso orchid blooming in a Canadian bog. He described it as "one of the most grotesquely beautiful wildflowers. It seems to try to overcome the terrible malformation of its flower with exquisitely beautiful coloring."

"Grotesque" or "malformed" they certainly aren't, but fairy slippers are clearly deceitful. Lacking nectar, the flowers offer no reward for potential pollinators. Still, bumblebees frequent them, carrying pollen on their backs from one flower to another. The question is, Why do bees continue to alight on these flowers, one after another, transferring pollen? After all, they are, in effect, wasting time they could use to visit nectar-rewarding blossoms on other plants. Only through careful observation did botanists realize that the bees flying to these early spring bloomers were newly emerged and inexperienced. To them, the colorful ornate fairy slippers appear to be flowers that *should* have nectar. After a day or so of fruitlessly crawling through ornate calypso flowers, bees learn to pass them up, but by then the flowers, with their dazzling appearance, have tricked them into pollinating.

CLIMATE CHANGE AND FAIRY SLIPPERS

Current global warming affects vegetation, especially plants such as fairy slippers that can tolerate only a narrow temperature range. Comparisons of their distribution today with records of locations over the past fifty years show striking range changes. Fairy slippers thrived in cedar swamps and forests as far south as central Michigan half a century ago; now, the plant's southern limit is more than one hundred miles closer to the pole.

The Wildflowers 🌿 149

Spotted Coralroot
Corallorhiza maculata (Raf.) Raf.

Orchid Family
Orchidaceae

Reddish brown leafless stems are topped with a dozen or so half-inch-wide flowers that remain inconspicuous until a shaft of sunlight strikes their gleaming white petals. The three sepals and the two upper petals are the same color as the stem; narrow with pointed tips, they arch over and around the larger pure white lower petal, which is dotted with rich magenta spots. A clump of foot-tall stems rises from an underground rhizome. After flowering, the dry hard stems persist through the winter.

A close relative, striped coralroot (*Corallorhiza striata*), bears whitish flowers that are candy striped with red lines. Blooming in early summer, both species frequent moist soils in the ponderosa pine, Douglas-fir, and spruce-fir zones. They exude a musklike scent that attracts small flies, bees, and beetles.

Corallorhiza, Latin for "coral root," describes the unusual underground system—a complicated mass of underground stems resembling pink sea coral. *Maculata* means "spotted"; and *striata*, "striped."

ORCHID FAMILY

With about twenty thousand species, the Orchid Family is one of the largest flowering plant families, along with the Sunflower and Grass families. Individual orchid plants, however, number far fewer than in those families.

The three sepals and two of the three petals are alike in shape and color, while the third petal—the lip—is larger and showier.

Orchid lips come in a variety of shapes and colors. They may be ornamented with lines or spots and often display hairs, scalloped edges, or fringes. Myriad elaborate variations of the lip open the way for coevolving specialized relationships with insects. Tropical orchid species often depend on a single insect for pollination. As conservation biologists point out, should that particular insect species disappear, the orchid will have no way of reproducing.

ORCHID REPRODUCTION

Orchid reproductive structures are unique. Stamens and style join in a column—a thickened structure that is often petal-like and colorful—and pollen is tightly packed into sticky, waxy masses that attach to the bodies of visiting insects to be carried away to other flowers.

Orchid seeds are small and light—so light they easily disperse in the wind, because, unlike the seeds of most flowering plants, they contain no food to sustain the germinating plant. Upon falling to the ground (or, in the tropics, onto a tree), an orchid seed must connect with a specific fungus that will provide minerals and nutrients in order to germinate, and it will maintain the fungal relationship for life. Thus, although a flower produces hundreds of thousands of seeds, few germinate.

Glossary

Anther the upper, pollen-bearing part of the stamen

Axil the upper angle where the leaf joins the stem

Bract a modified leaf at the base of a flower or flower cluster

Bulb an enlarged underground stem of fleshy scales

Corm a thickened, vertical underground stem

Corolla the collective name for the petals of a flower

Floret the modified flower of the Aster Family
     Disk floret a small, tubular flower of the Aster Family
     Ray floret a strap-shaped flower of the Aster Family

Flower or floral head a compact cluster of florets

Gland a cell or group of cells that secretes a sticky or
     oily substance

Herbaceous not woody

Inflorescence a flower cluster

Involucre the whorl of bracts subtending the flower head

Lance-shaped longer than wide, with the widest point
     below the middle

Leaf the photosynthetic organ of a plant
     Alternate leaves leaves borne singly at each node
     Basal leaves leaves arising from the base of the stem
     Compound leaf leaf blade divided into separate leaflets
     Opposite leaves leaves borne in pairs at each node
     Whorled leaves three or more leaves arising at each node

Nectary the nectar-producing organ

Node the position on the stem where leaves or branches originate

Ovary the lower part of the pistil where the ovules are fertilized
     and develop into seeds

Ovule unfertilized seed within the ovary

Pistil the female reproductive organ, consisting of the ovary and stigma connected by a slender style

Pod a dry fruit that splits along the edges

Pollen the microscopic products of the stamens that fertilize the ovules

Rhizome a horizontal underground stem

Sepal one element of the outer whorl of leaflike structures surrounding the corolla

Stamen the male reproductive organ, consisting of an anther supported by a filament

Stigma the area at the tip of the pistil that receives pollen and guides it to the ovules

Style the slender part of the pistil between the ovary and stigma

Tepals petals and sepals that are indistinguishable from each other

Tuber a thick, fleshy underground stem

Umbel a flower cluster with stalks of equal length radiating from a common center
Compound umbel a cluster of small umbels united into a large umbel

Suggested References

The following guides are useful companion volumes to *Mountain Wildflowers of the Southern Rockies.*

Craighead, John J., Frank C. Craighead Jr., and Ray J. Davis. 1991. *A Field Guide to Rocky Mountain Wildflowers: Northern Arizona and New Mexico to British Columbia.* Boston: Houghton Mifflin.

Dolan, Merrille. 1996. *Favorite Flowers of the Cumbres and Toltec.* Albuquerque: Dragonfly Press.

Dunmire, William W., and Gail D. Tierney. 1995. *Wild Plants of the Pueblo Province: Exploring Ancient and Enduring Uses.* Santa Fe: Museum of New Mexico Press.

———. 1997. *Wild Plants and Native Peoples of the Four Corners.* Santa Fe: Museum of New Mexico Press.

Guennel, G. K. 2004. *Guide to Colorado Wildflowers, vol. 2: Mountains.* 2nd ed. Englewood, CO: Westcliffe Publishers.

Ivey, Robert Dewitt. 2003. *Flowering Plants of New Mexico.* 4th ed. Albuquerque: Author.

Julyan, Robert, and Mary Steuver, eds. 2005. *Field Guide to the Sandia Mountains.* Albuquerque: University of New Mexico Press.

Robertson, Leigh. 1999. *Southern Rocky Mountain Wildflowers.* Guilford, CT: Globe Pequot Press.

Tierney, Gail D. 1983. *Roadside Plants of Northern New Mexico.* Santa Fe: Lightning Tree.

Selected Bibliography

Abrahamson, Warren G., ed. 1989. *Plant–Animal Interactions.*
New York: McGraw-Hill.

Allen, Robert B., Robert K. Peet, and William L. Baker. 1991.
"Gradient Analysis of Latitudinal Variation in Southern
Rocky Mountain Forests." *Journal of Biogeography* 18:123–139.

Allred, Kelly W., ed. Database. Available at http://web.nmsu.edu
/~kallred/herbweb/Working%20Index.pdf.

Bailey, Liberty Hyde. 1976. *Hortus Third: A Concise Dictionary of
Plants Cultivated in the United States.* New York: Macmillan.

Brown, David E. 1982. "Biotic Communities of the American
Southwest—United States and Mexico." *Desert Plants* 4:1–4.

Brummitt, R. K., and C. E. Powell. 1992. *Authors of Plant Names:
A List of Authors of Scientific Names of Plants, with
Recommended Standard Forms of Their Names, Including
Abbreviations.* London: Royale Botanic Gardens, Kew.

Cronquist, Arthur. 1972. *Intermountain Flora: Vascular Plants of the
Intermountain West, U.S.A.* New York: Hafner Publishing Co.

Dick-Peddie, William A. 1993. *New Mexico Vegetation: Past, Present
and Future.* Albuquerque: University of New Mexico Press.

Dunmire, William W. 2004. *Gardens of New Spain: How
Mediterranean Plants and Foods Changed America.*
Austin: University of Texas Press.

Emory, William H. 1987. *Report on the United States and Mexican
Boundary Survey.* Austin: Texas State Historical Association.

Ewan, Joseph Andorfer. 1950. *Rocky Mountain Naturalists.*
Denver: University of Denver Press.

Ewan, Joseph Andorfer, and Nesta Dunn. 1981. *Biographical Dictionary of Rocky Mountain Naturalists: A Guide to the Writings and Collections of Botanists, Zoologists, Geologists, and Photographers, 1682–1932.* Utrecht: Bohn, Scheltema and Holkema.

Faegri, Knut, and L. van der Pigl. 1979. *The Principals of Pollination Ecology.* 3rd ed. Oxford: Pergamon Press.

Flora of North America Editorial Committee, ed. 1993–. *Flora of North America, North of Mexico.* New York: Oxford University Press.

Grant, Verne, and Karen A. Grant. 1965. *Flower Pollination in the Phlox Family.* New York: Columbia University Press.

Harborne, Jeffry B., and Herbert Baxte, eds. 1996. *Dictionary of Plant Toxins.* New York: Wiley.

Harris, James G., and Melinda Woolf. 2001. *Plant Identification Terminology: An Illustrated Glossary.* 2nd ed. Spring Lake, UT: Spring Lake Publishers.

Hyam, R., and R. Pankhurst. 1995. *Plants and Their Names: A Concise Dictionary.* Oxford: Oxford University Press.

Isely, Duane. 1994. *One Hundred and One Botanists.* Ames: Iowa State University Press.

Judd, Walter S. 2002. *Plant Systemics: A Phylogenetic Approach.* Sunderland, MA: Sinauer Associates.

Kartesz, John T. 1994. *A Synonymized Checklist of the Vascular Flora of the United States, Canada, and Greenland.* Portland, OR: Timber Press.

Martin, William C., and Charles R. Hutchins. 1980. *A Flora of New Mexico.* Vaduz: J. Cramer.

Moerman, Daniel E. 1998. *Native American Ethnobotany*. Portland, OR: Timber Press.

Peet, Robert K. 1981. "Forest Vegetation of the Colorado Front Range." *Vegetatio* 45:3 75.

Proctor, Michael C. F., Peter Yeo, and Andrew Lack. 1996. *The Natural History of Pollination*. Portland, OR: Timber Press.

Stearn, William T. 1995. *Botanical Latin: History, Grammar, Syntax, Terminology, and Vocabulary*. 4th ed. Portland, OR: Timber Press.

U.S. Department of Agriculture, Forest Service. 1988. *Range Plant Handbook*. New York: Dover Publications.

U.S. Department of Agriculture, Natural Resources Conservation Service. 2006. "The PLANTS Database." Available at http://plants.usda.gov. National Plant Data Center, Baton Rouge, LA 70874-4490.

Vines, Robert A. 1960. *Trees, Shrubs, and Woody Vines of the Southwest*. Austin: University of Texas Press.

Weber, William A., and Ronald C. Wittmann. 2001a. *Colorado Flora: Eastern Slope*. 3rd ed. Boulder: University Press of Colorado.

———. 2001b. *Colorado Flora: Western Slope*. 3rd ed. Boulder: University Press of Colorado.

About the Authors

Senior author Carolyn Dodson became aware of the need for this book while teaching wildflower identification classes at the University of New Mexico (UNM) Department of Continuing Education. She has a master's degree in botany from City University of New York and is retired from the faculty of the UNM General Library. During her twenty-five years in the Southwest she has hiked and camped throughout the Southern Rockies, studying and photographing the wildflowers. She is an active member of the New Mexico Native Plant Society and the Council on Botanical and Horticultural Libraries.

Bill Dunmire's interest in wild plants developed during his twenty-eight-year career with the National Park Service, most of which was spent as a park naturalist in parks across the country, and later as a field biologist in New Mexico for The Nature Conservancy. He coauthored *Wild Plants of the Pueblo Province* and *Wild Plants and Native Peoples of the Four Corners* with Gail D. Tierney and authored *Gardens of New Spain: How Mediterranean Plants and Foods Changed America*. His degrees in biology are from the University of California, Berkeley, and he currently is an Associate in Biology at the University of New Mexico.

Photography Credits

The following photographs are by Carolyn Dodson:
p. ii (all three); p. iii (all three); pp. 2, 4, 5, 6, 9, 10, 11, 12, 14, 16, 17, 18, 19, 20, 21, 22, 23, 24, 25, 28, 30, 31, 32, 36, 37, 38, 40, 41, 42, 44, 45, 46, 48, 49, 50, 51, 52, 53, 56, 57, 58, 60, 61, 62, 64, 68, 69, 71, 72, 74, 75, 76, 77, 78, 79, 80, 82, 83, 84, 85, 86, 89, 90, 92, 93, 94, 96, 97, 98, 99, 101, 103, 105, 107, 108, 109, 111, 112, 113, 114, 115, 116, 117, 118, 119, 120, 121, 122, 123, 125, 126, 127, 128, 129, 130, 131, 132, 133, 134, 135, 136, 139, 140, 141, 142, 144, 145, 146, 148, 150, 151; all back cover.

The following photographs are by William W. Dunmire:
front cover; p. xi; pp. 8, 15, 26, 27, 34, 35, 47, 54, 55, 59, 66, 67, 70, 81, 88, 100, 102, 104, 110, 124, 137, 138, 147, 149.

Index

hawk moths, 7
heart-leaf buttercup, 12
heart-leaved bittercress, 36–37
Heath Family, 40–41;
    characteristics of, 40
Helenium hoopesii. See
    Hymenoxys hoopesii
Helianthella quinquenervis, 132
Heliomeris multiflora, 130–31
hemlock: poison, 75;
    water, 74–75
Heracleum maximum, 76–77
Heterotheca spp., 131
hoary evening-primrose, 68
holly-grape. *See* grape-holly
honeysuckle, ruby. *See* scarlet
    gilia
Honeysuckle Family, 114–17;
    characteristics of, 115
Hooker, William, 103
Hooker's evening-primrose,
    68–69
Hoopes, Thomas, 133
horsemint. *See* beebalm
Hummingbird, Rufous, 89, 111
hummingbird flower. *See* scarlet
    penstemon
hummingbirds, 7, 89, 101, 102,
    104, 111
Hymenoxys hoopesii, 132–33
Hypericum perforatum, 29
Hypericum scouleri, 28–29
hyssop, giant, 98–99

Iltis, Hugh, 85
Indian paintbrush, 102–3
Indian Pipe Family, 44–45

Indians: and dye plants, 15, 95;
    and fiber plants, 70; and
    food plants, 35, 66, 76,
    105, 139, 141, 143. *See also*
    food plants; and medicinal
    plants, 15, 19, 27, 41, 89, 94,
    101, 123. *See also* medicinal
    plants; and paint plants, 35;
    and toxic plants, 75, 144,
    147
Indian spinach. *See* Rocky
    Mountain beeplant
indicator plants, 61
Ipomopsis aggregata, 88–89
Iridaceae, 146–47
iris, Rocky Mountain, 146–47
Iris Family, 146–47;
    characteristics of, 146
Iris missouriensis, 146–147

Jacob's ladder, 90–91; showy, 90
James, Edwin, 7

Kalm, Peter, 87
king's crown, 50
kinnickinnick. *See* bearberry
Klamath weed, 29
Kuntze, Karl, 85

Labiatae. See *Lamiaceae*
Lamiaceae, 98–101
languid ladies. *See* bluebells
larkspur, Barbey, 10–11
Latin plant names.
    See binomial system
leaf: compound, 117; function,
    51; movement, 63
Lemmon, John Gill, 81

Rose Family, 54–59; characteristics of, 55
Rubiaceae, 120–21
Rubia tinctoria, 121
ruby honeysuckle. *See* scarlet gilia

saffron, 147
sagebrush, 27
Sambucus racemosa, 116–17
saprophytes, 44
Saxifragaceae, 52–53
Saxifraga rhomboidea, 52–53
saxifrage: diamondleaf, 52–53; snowball. *See* diamondleaf saxifrage
Saxifrage Family, 52–53; characteristics of, 53
scarlet bugler. *See* scarlet penstemon
scarlet gilia, 88–89, 110
scarlet penstemon, 110–11
Scrophulariaceae, 102–13
seed dispersal, 55, 72–73, 151
sego lily, 139
self-fertilization, 49
Senecio bigelovii, 134–35
shade: and plants, 37
shooting star, 46–47
showy daisy, 128–29
showy goldeneye, 130–31
showy Jacob's ladder, 90
showy milkweed, 86–87
Sidalcea candida, 30–31
sidebells, 43
Silene acaulis, 22–23
silverweed cinquefoil, 56–57
silvery lupine, 62–63

skunkleaf. *See* Jacob's ladder
sky pilot, 90
skyrocket. *See* scarlet gilia
Small, John, 25
Smilacina, 142
Snapdragon Family, 102–13; characteristics of, 106
sneezeweed, orange, 132–33
snowball saxifrage. *See* diamondleaf saxifrage
snow buttercup, 12
snow lily. *See* fawn lily
Solomon's seal: false, 142; star, 142–43
Southern Rockies: delineated, xi–xii; map of, x
spotted coralroot, 150–51
spruce-fir zone, xii
St. Johnswort, 28–29
St. Johnswort Family, 28–29; characteristics of, 28
star Solomon's seal, 142–43
stemless meadow thistle, 126
Stephen H. Long Expedition, 7
Stonecrop Family, 50–51; characteristics of, 51
strawberry, wild, 54–55
striped coralroot, 150
succulents, 51
sulphur flower, 26–27
sunflower, nodding, 132
Sunflower Family. See *Asteraceae*
Swertia radiata. See *Frasera speciosa*
synchronized flowering, 83

Texas bluebonnet, 63
Thermopsis montanus, 64–65